Language in use
INTERMEDIATE

Self-Study Workbook
with answer key

ADRIAN DOFF & CHRISTOPHER JONES

CAMBRIDGE
UNIVERSITY PRESS

PUBLISHED BY THE PRESS SYNDICATE OF THE UNIVERSITY OF CAMBRIDGE
The Pitt Building, Trumpington Street, Cambridge, United Kingdom

CAMBRIDGE UNIVERSITY PRESS
The Edinburgh Building, Cambridge CB2 2RU, UK   www.cup.cam.ac.uk
40 West 20th Street, New York, NY 10011–4211, USA   www.cup.org
10 Stamford Road, Oakleigh, Melbourne 3166, Australia
Ruiz de Alarcón 13, 28014 Madrid, Spain

© Cambridge University Press 1994

This book is in copyright. Subject to statutory exception
and to the provisions of relevant collective licensing agreements,
no reproduction of any part may take place without
the written permission of Cambridge University Press.

First published 1994
Eighth printing 1999

Printed in the United Kingdom at the University Press, Cambridge

ISBN 0 521 43554 4 Self-study Workbook with Answer Key
ISBN 0 521 43555 2 Self-study Workbook
ISBN 0 521 43552 8 Classroom Book
ISBN 0 521 43553 6 Teacher's Book
ISBN 0 521 43560 9 Class Cassette Set
ISBN 0 521 43561 7 Self-study Cassette Set

Split editions:
ISBN 0 521 43556 0 Self-study Workbook A with Answer Key
ISBN 0 521 43557 9 Self-study Workbook B with Answer Key
ISBN 0 521 43562 5 Self-study Cassette A
ISBN 0 521 43563 3 Self-study Cassette B
ISBN 0 521 43558 7 Classroom Book A
ISBN 0 521 43559 5 Classroom Book B

Contents

	To the student	page 4
	Guide to units	6
Unit 1	Regular events	10
Unit 2	Around the house	14
Unit 3	Past events	18
Unit 4	Money	22
Unit 5	Obligation	26
Unit 6	On holiday	30
	Review	34
Unit 7	Past and present	36
Unit 8	At your service	40
Unit 9	Imagining	44
Unit 10	Describing things	48
Unit 11	The future	52
Unit 12	Accidents	56
	Review	60
Unit 13	Comparing and evaluating	62
Unit 14	The media	66
Unit 15	Recent events	70
Unit 16	Teaching and learning	74
Unit 17	Narration	78
Unit 18	Breaking the law	82
	Review	86
Unit 19	Up to now	88
Unit 20	In your lifetime	92
Unit 21	Finding out	96
Unit 22	Speaking personally	100
Unit 23	The unreal past	104
Unit 24	Life on Earth	108
	Review	112
	Tapescripts	114
	Answer key	120
	Phrasal verbs reference section	136

To the student

This Workbook contains exercises for you to do on your own.

Each Workbook unit begins with grammar or vocabulary exercises, which give extra practice in the language you have learned in class.

In addition, there are self-study exercises which help you to develop particular skills in English. These are:
- Listening skills (in each unit)
- Reading skills (in each Grammar unit)
- Writing skills (in each Vocabulary unit)
- Pronunciation (in Grammar units)
- Phrasal verbs (in Vocabulary units)

After every six units, there is a Review test.

There are also two Self-study Cassettes that go with the Workbook. You will need to use these for the Listening and Pronunciation exercises, some of the Phrasal verbs exercises, and the Dictation exercises in the Review tests.

Here is a short description of the exercises in the Workbook:

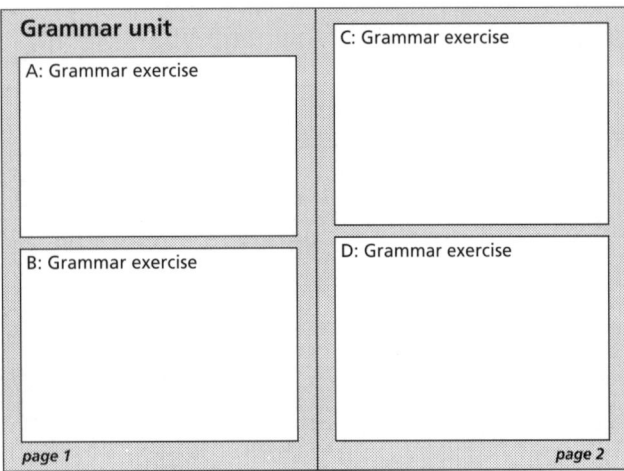
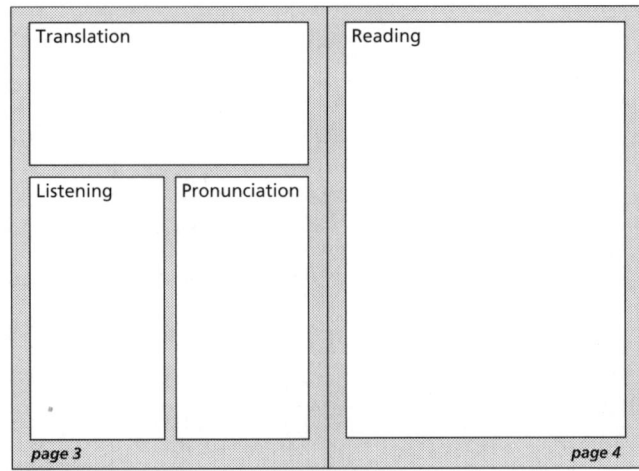

Grammar exercises
The grammar exercises give practice in the main structures of the unit. They usually include one puzzle or word game, and sometimes one freer exercise. There are three or four grammar exercises in each unit.

Translation
This section contains sentences for you to translate into your own language – and then back into English.

Listening
These are short listening tasks, which give you a chance to listen to natural English in your own time. Usually these are similar to one of the activities from the Classroom Book.

Pronunciation
These exercises give practice in pronunciation, stress and intonation.

Reading
This section contains reading tasks based on a variety of short texts. These include magazine and newspaper articles, letters, games and stories.

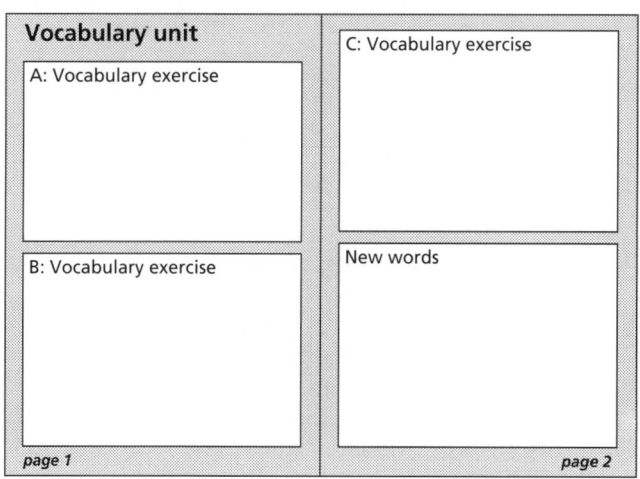
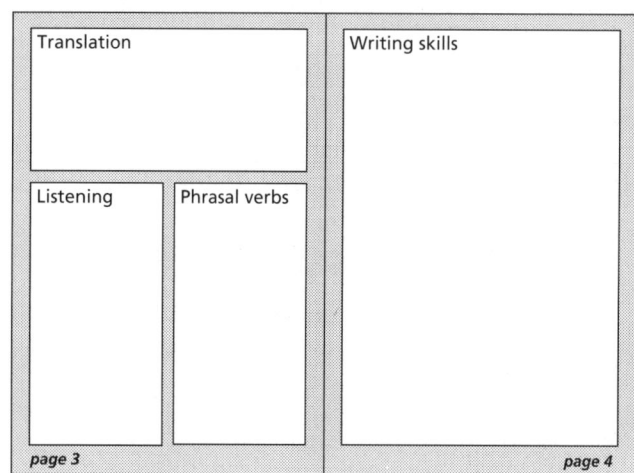

Vocabulary exercises
The vocabulary exercises give practice in the main vocabulary areas of the unit. They usually include one puzzle or word game, and sometimes one freer exercise. There are two or three vocabulary exercises in each unit.

New words
This is a space for you to write down new words from the unit, together with your own notes and examples.

Translation
This section contains sentences for you to translate into your own language – and then back into English.

Listening
These are short listening tasks, which give you a chance to listen to natural English in your own time. Usually these are similar to one of the activities from the Classroom Book.

Phrasal verbs
These exercises teach a range of common phrasal verbs. You will sometimes need the cassette.

Writing skills
These exercises teach intermediate level writing skills, which include punctuation, using pronouns, joining sentences and organising ideas.

Guide to units

Self-study Workbook | Classroom Book

1 Regular events

Grammar exercises
Listening: *Personality types*
Pronunciation: *The sound /ə/*
Reading: *How to saw someone in half*

Talking about regular events and actions; talking about current activities
Grammar: Present simple active & passive; frequency expressions; Present continuous

2 Around the house

Vocabulary exercises
Listening: *A Spanish family*
Phrasal verbs: *Introduction*
Writing skills: *Punctuation: joining sentences*

Vocabulary: behaviour in the home; household jobs & appliances; features of rooms
Reading and listening activity: *Snow house*

3 Past events

Grammar exercises
Listening: *Childhood memories*
Pronunciation: *Reduced and full forms*
Reading: *Two terrible tales*

Talking about past events and actions; saying when things happened
Grammar: Past simple and continuous; past time expressions; subject & object questions; Past simple passive

4 Money

Vocabulary exercises
Listening: *A waste of money*
Phrasal verbs: *Intransitive verbs (1)*
Writing skills: *Reference: pronouns*

Vocabulary: cost and value; using money; expenses, bills & taxes
Reading and listening activity: *Can you make a million?*

5 Obligation

Grammar exercises
Listening: *School rules*
Pronunciation: *Contracted forms*
Reading: *Three word games*

Obligation and permission in the present and past; freedom from obligation
Grammar: (don't) have to; (not) allowed to; can('t); make & let; freedom from obligation structures

6 On holiday

Vocabulary exercises
Listening: *Going home*
Phrasal verbs: *Intransitive verbs (2)*
Writing skills: *Subject and object relative clauses*

Vocabulary: types of holiday; holiday activities; holiday equipment; festivals & celebrations
Reading and listening activity: *Culture shock*

Review Units 1–6

Self-study Workbook	Classroom Book
7 Past and present	
Grammar exercises Listening: *Changed lives* Pronunciation: *Syllables and stress* Reading: *Two childhoods*	Habitual actions in the past; describing changes; preparations **Grammar:** used to; Past simple; Present perfect active and passive; not any more/longer
8 At your service	
Vocabulary exercises Listening: *On the phone* Phrasal verbs: *Transitive verbs (1)* Writing skills: *Punctuation: direct speech*	**Vocabulary:** having things done; using public services; evaluating services **Reading and listening activity:** *Jobs we love to hate*
9 Imagining	
Grammar exercises Listening: *What would you do?* Pronunciation: *Linking words: consonant + vowel* Reading: *My perfect weekend*	Imagining things differently from the way they are; making wishes **Grammar:** would; second conditionals; I wish + would / could / Past tense
10 Describing things	
Vocabulary exercises Listening: *Things for sale* Phrasal verbs: *Transitive verbs (2)* Writing skills: *Reference:* this *and* which	**Vocabulary:** describing objects by appearance and purpose; buying & selling **Reading and listening activity:** *Great ideas?*
11 The future	
Grammar exercises Listening: *When I'm 60 ...* Pronunciation: *Stress in sentences* Reading: *Crossing the Sahara*	Making predictions; hopes & expectations; giving reasons for predictions **Grammar:** will/might; hope & expect; Future continuous; Future perfect; linking words
12 Accidents	
Vocabulary exercises Listening: *Narrow escapes* Phrasal verbs: *Transitive verbs (3)* Writing skills: *Joining ideas: clauses and phrases*	**Vocabulary:** describing accidents and injuries; dealing with emergencies; road accidents **Reading and listening activity:** *You're on your own*
Review Units 7–12	

Self-study Workbook	Classroom Book
13 Comparing and evaluating	
Grammar exercises Listening: *Living in Britain* Pronunciation: *Linking words: consonant + consonant* Reading: *Left-handedness*	Comparing things; comparing the way people do things; criticising and complaining Grammar: comparative adjectives and adverbs; (not) as ... as ...; too & enough
14 The media	
Vocabulary exercises Listening: *Media habits* Phrasal verbs: *Double meanings* Writing skills: *Similarities*	Vocabulary: newspapers and magazines, and their contents; types of TV programme Reading and listening activity: *Easy listening*
15 Recent events	
Grammar exercises Listening: *What has happened?* Pronunciation: *Changing stress* Reading: *Personal letters*	Announcing news; giving and asking about details; talking about recent activities Grammar: Present perfect simple active & passive; Past simple; Present perfect continuous
16 Teaching and learning	
Vocabulary exercises Listening: *Three school subjects* Phrasal verbs: *Prepositional verbs (1)* Writing skills: *Letter writing*	Vocabulary: learning things at school; skills and abilities; education systems Reading and listening activity: *Improve your memory*
17 Narration	
Grammar exercises Listening: *Locked in!* Pronunciation: *Linking words with /w/ or /j/* Reading: *Strange – but true?*	Flashbacks in narration; changes in the past; reported speech and thought Grammar: Past perfect tense; reported speech structures
18 Breaking the law	
Vocabulary exercises Listening: *A case of fraud* Phrasal verbs: *Prepositional verbs (2)* Writing skills: *Defining and non-defining relative clauses*	Vocabulary: types of crime; types of punishment; courts and trials Reading and listening activity: *Detective Shadow*
Review Units 13–18	

Self-study Workbook	Classroom Book
19 Up to now	
Grammar exercises Listening: *Favourite things* Pronunciation: *Stress and suffixes* Reading: *Four logic puzzles*	Saying when things started; saying how long things have (or haven't) been going on **Grammar:** Present perfect simple/continuous + for/since; negative duration structures
20 In your lifetime	
Vocabulary exercises Listening: *Birth and marriage* Phrasal verbs: *Three-word verbs (1)* Writing skills: *Joining ideas: showing what's coming next*	**Vocabulary:** birth, marriage and death; age groups; age and the law **Reading and listening activity:** *A Good Boy, Griffith*
21 Finding out	
Grammar exercises Listening: *Phone conversation* Pronunciation: *Changing tones* Reading: *A bit of luck*	Asking for information; reporting questions; checking **Grammar:** information questions; indirect questions; reported questions; question tags
22 Speaking personally	
Vocabulary exercises Listening: *James Bond films* Phrasal verbs: *Three-word verbs (2)* Writing skills: *Sequence: unexpected events*	**Vocabulary:** ways of describing feelings; positive & negative reactions **Reading and listening activity:** *What's in a smile*
23 The unreal past	
Grammar exercises Listening: *A better place* Pronunciation: *Common suffixes* Reading: *If things had been different …*	Imagining what would have happened in different circumstances; expressing regret **Grammar:** would have done; 2nd and 3rd conditionals; I wish + Past perfect; should(n't) have done
24 Life on Earth	
Vocabulary exercises Listening: *How green are you?* Phrasal verbs: *Review* Writing skills: *Organising ideas*	**Vocabulary:** environmental problems and solutions; endangered species **Reading and listening activity:** *The Doomsday Asteroid*
Review Units 19–24	

1 Regular events

A Explanations

Complete the sentences below with information from the box.
Add *don't*, *doesn't* or 3rd person *-s* if necessary.

1 I'm a Muslim. I *don't drink alcohol.*
2 Vegetarians ....
3 In Switzerland, most people ....
4 Roman Catholic priests ....
5 She's unemployed. She ....
6 British drivers ....
7 The President of the USA ....
8 The sun ....
9 He's illiterate. He ....
10 Banks ....

> drive on the left of the road
> live in the White House
> speak German
> open on New Year's Day
> ~~drink alcohol~~
> rise in the east
> eat meat
> know how to read and write
> get married
> have a job

B Frequency

Change these sentences so that they are true for you.

Example:

I make about five phone calls a day.
I make about 10 phone calls a day.
or *I make a phone call about three times a week.*

1 I make about five phone calls a day.

   ....

2 I wash my hair twice a week.

   ....

3 I go to the cinema about once every two months.

   ....

4 I write about three letters a week.

   ....

5 I go shopping three times a week.

   ....

6 I eat chips every day.

   ....

7 I clean my shoes once a month.

   ....

C Present simple passive

Which bubbles go with which products? Rewrite each sentence using the Present simple passive.

> **Present simple passive**
> is/are + past participle
> They make it → It's made
> We don't sell it → It isn't sold

Bubbles:
- All the best schools use them.
- We make them from real leather.
- We design them for your comfort.
- Hollywood stars eat them.
- We seal in all the flavour.
- We illustrate them in full colour.
- We use the finest ingredients.
- Experts write them.
- We guarantee them for 12 months.

Ice-cream
All the flavour is sealed in
The finest ingredients are used
It's eaten by Hollywood stars

Shoes
They made from real leather
They are designed for our comfort
It's guaranteed for 12 months

Story-books
They are used from all best schools
They are illustrated in full colours
It's written by experts

NAPOLI ice-cream — The coolest taste in the world

KLASSIKA — QUALITY SHOES FOR MEN AND WOMEN

Easy Reads — Good stories for learners of English

D At the moment

For each situation, write two or three sentences saying what's happening. Use the ideas in the boxes to help you.

1 It's wonderful having my parents to stay. *They're cooking all the meals, and they're spending a lot of time with the children.*

   cook / children / do the washing / paint

2 The weather's incredibly hot at the moment. *Everyone's wearing shorts and T-shirts,*

   shorts / sunbathe / ice-cream / sit outside

3 I'm really enjoying being at home with the 'flu.

TRANSLATION

Translate into your own language:

1 – How often do you clean your teeth?
  – Twice a day. Once in the morning, and once at night.

2 Every day, one person is killed in a road accident and 20 people are injured.

3 – What do you do?
  – I'm a teacher, but just at the moment I'm working as a waiter.

Now cover up the left-hand side, and translate your sentences back into English.

LISTENING: Personality types

1 You will hear someone talking about how he spends his time. Listen and mark these sentences ✓ or ✗.

   a He's often invited to parties.
   b He likes going to concerts and operas.
   c He doesn't see his children much in the evenings.
   d His children like going to museums and art galleries.
   e He often takes his children camping.
   f He often takes work home to do in the evening.

2 Listen again and decide what kind of person the speaker is. Give him a score from 0 to 10 for each of the categories below (0 = not at all, 10 = a lot).

A sociable type	
A culture-vulture	
A home-lover	
An outdoor type	
A workaholic	

PRONUNCIATION: The sound /ə/

1 Listen to these words on the tape. Each circle marks a /ə/ sound. Notice that this sound can be spelt in many different ways.

fath(er)   col(our)   pr(o)nunciati(o)n
th(e)   (a)bout   Arg(e)ntin(a)

2 Listen to these phrases and circle the sound /ə/ every time you hear it.

a Russian tractor
a million dollars
a famous conductor
a colour photograph
the Argentinian Government

3 Where do you think the /ə/ sound comes in these sentences?

   a I'm reading a brilliant American novel.
   b My sister's attending a conference in London.
   c Will you answer the question?
   d Fortunately the driver wasn't injured in the accident.
   e My cousin's picture is in today's newspaper.

Now listen and practise saying the sentences.

READING: How to saw someone in half

A The magician and his assistant take a large saw, and start sawing through the box. They keep sawing until the box is completely cut in two.

B The magician spins the table around in a circle, so that the audience can see the box from all sides.

C A large wooden table is pushed onto the stage. On the table there is a large wooden box with a lid. The box has holes for the victim's head, arms and legs.

D The magician pushes the box together again, removes the metal plates and unlocks the lid. He then opens up the lid, and the victim gets out of the box – in one piece.

E The lid of the box is opened, and his 'victim' gets inside. She puts her head, arms and legs through the holes, so that the audience can see them. Then the lid is closed, and locked.

F Two metal plates are inserted into the box, one on each side of the cut, and the two halves of the box are pulled apart. The victim, who appears to be cut in two, smiles and moves her hands and feet.

G The magician tells the audience that because the trick is extremely dangerous, there's an ambulance waiting outside the theatre. A medical team, in uniform, is brought in and stands at the back of the hall.

1 The pictures show seven stages of a trick in which a magician saws someone in half. Match the texts with the pictures.

2 How do you think the trick is done? Think about it, then read the solution. Were you right?

How it's done

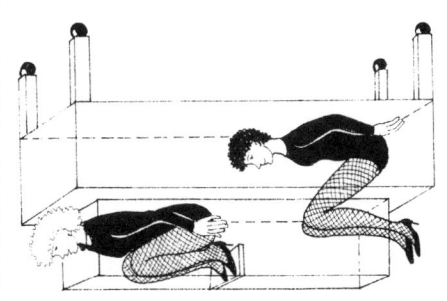

There is not one 'victim', but two – A and B. When the trick begins, B is already hidden inside the table. When the magician spins the table round, there are a few moments when A's legs cannot be seen by the audience. She quickly pulls her legs out of the holes, brings them right back, and places them against a ledge in the lid of the box. At the same time, B lifts her legs up into the box and out through the leg-hole. The magician can now safely cut the box in two.

Unit 1 Regular events

2 Around the house

A Good housekeeping

Write the answers to the clues in the diagrams.

Don't (16 ▶) your things (4 ▶) all over the floor: put them (2 ▼)!

Hey! Someone's (8 ▶) up all the hot (14 ▼)!

Don't (16 ▶) the lights on when you go out: (5 ▶) them off. Remember that lights (12 ▶) electricity – and electricity is expensive.

My sister's room is always in a terrible (9 ▶), so (10 ▼) can never find anything. I'm different. I like to (11 ▶) my room (7 ▼), so that I know (3 ▶) everything is.

My brother always stays up very (17 ▶), playing loud music. He (9 ▼) such a lot of noise that the rest of us can't get to sleep.

When we've finished eating a (15 ▼), we always (13 ▼) away everything from the table and (6 ▼) the dishes. We like to keep the kitchen nice and (1 ▼).

B Labour-saving devices

1 What are the names of these labour-saving devices?

a *sewing machine*
b ....
c ....
d ....
e ....
f ....
g ....
h ....

2 Imagine you could only afford *three* of the objects. Which three would you choose, and why?

....
....
....
....

C Features of rooms

Look at the picture of the room, and answer the questions. Use the words in the box to help you.

bare	patterned	statue
comfortable	plant	tasteful
elegant	rug	vase
floorboards	sofa	wallpaper

1 What furniture is there in the room?

....
....
....
....

2 What can you say about the walls and floor? ....
....

3 What ornaments are there in the room? ....
....

4 What about the view? ....
....

5 What's your general impression of the room? ....
....

New words

Use this space to write down new words from the unit, with your own notes and examples.

....
....
....
....
....
....
....
....
....
....
....
....
....
....

Unit 2 Around the house

TRANSLATION

Translate into your own language:

1 He's terribly untidy. He never puts anything away, and he never does any washing up.

Er ist sehr unordentlich. Nie räumt er auf und er wäscht nie ab.

2 Don't forget to switch the lights off when you go out.

Vergiß nie, alle Lichter auszuschalten, wenn Du das Haus verläßt.

3 The room faces south, and has a lovely view of the sea.

Das Zimmer zeigt gen Süden und bietet einen herrlichen Blick auf das Meer.

Now cover up the left-hand side, and translate your sentences back into English.

LISTENING: A Spanish family

You will hear someone talking about family life in Spain.

1 🔲 In the first part he talks about his own childhood. Listen and choose the correct answers.

His mother was born | just before / just after | the war. She

had a | traditional / modern | view of her place in the

home. She | did all the housework herself. / taught her children to help her.

When he left home, he was | able / unable | to look after himself.

2 🔲 In the second part, he talks about his brothers' families. Who does the things below in these families – the man, the woman, or both? (Write M, W or B.)

a ☐ playing with the children
b ☐ reading the children stories
c ☐ changing babies' nappies
d ☐ doing the housework
e ☐ earning the money
f ☐ managing the money for the home

PHRASAL VERBS: Introduction

1 Phrasal verbs have two parts: a *verb* (e.g. *make, go, get*) and one (or sometimes two) *'small words'* (e.g. *on, up, out, with*) which go with the verb. Compare these examples:

'Normal' verbs
try   I *tried* to phone you this morning.
break   He dropped the plate and it *broke*.
catch   She just *caught* the last bus.

Phrasal verbs
try on   I *tried* the shoes *on*, but they didn't fit.
break down   The bus *broke down* and we had to walk.
catch up with You go ahead – I'll *catch up with* you later.

2 The 'small words' in phrasal verbs are important, because they completely change the meaning. For example, *get up* = get out of bed; *get away* = escape; *get on with* someone = like being with them.

All these sentences have phrasal verbs with *look*. Can you guess what they mean? Match them with the meanings in the box. Use a dictionary to help you.

| have a view of | raise your head | visit |
| try to find | find the meaning of | be careful |

a *Look out* – the path's very slippery.
b I'll have to *look* that word *up* in my dictionary.
c His room *looks out* on a busy main road.
d I'll *look* you *up* if I come to London.
e I said 'Hello' but he didn't even *look up*.
f They're *looking for* a flat in the town centre.

There is a Phrasal verbs reference section on the last page of the book.

Unit 2 Around the house

WRITING SKILLS: Punctuation: joining sentences

1 **Look at these sentences.**

Incorrect

I'm learning French, I can't speak it well.

I was under 18, I couldn't get into the film.

I went to see him that evening, it was the last time I saw him alive.

People here are really friendly, they're always smiling and laughing.

There are two things I love, cheeseburgers and vanilla ice-cream.

Correct

I'm learning French but I can't speak it well.

I was under 18, so I couldn't get into the film.

I went to see him that evening; it was the last time I saw him alive.

People here are really friendly – they're always smiling and laughing.

There are two things I love: cheeseburgers and vanilla ice-cream.

To join two parts of a sentence, we can use

- a linking word (*and*, *but*, *or*)
- a comma plus a linking word (*so*, *but*, *because*, etc.)
- a semi-colon (;) (to join parts of a sentence without using a linking word)
- a dash (–) (in informal writing, such as a letter to a friend)
- a colon (:) to introduce a list.

2 **Join these sentences by adding a linking word and/or punctuation to each box.**

a Switzerland has four official languages [   ] French, German, Italian and Romansch.

b I couldn't get in touch with you [   ] I didn't know your address.

c The igloo is below ground level [   ] there's plenty of room to stand up.

d I wish you were here [   ] I'm sure you'd really like it.

e It was a beautiful sunset [   ] the sky changed from yellow to pink [   ] then slowly to purple.

3 **Rewrite this advertisement so that it contains five sentences. Add punctuation, linking words and capital letters where necessary.**

our new range of kitchen tables comes in three exciting colours pale green lemon yellow and fiery red the tables are made of tough plastic they're almost impossible to scratch or burn the surface is easy to wipe clean after your meal just fill in the form below send it to us then sit back and relax we'll deliver the table to you within a week you can pay in any way you like in cash by cheque or by credit card if you're not completely delighted with your table you can send it back you won't owe us a penny

....
....
....
....
....
....

3 Past events

A Short stories

Complete these stories so that each one says
– what was happening
– what happened
– what happened next.

1 I was having a shower *when I slipped on the soap* .... and banged my head on the wall.

2 .... when I ran out of petrol, so I ....

....

3 The waiter was just putting my meal on the table ....

...., so I had to go home and change my clothes.

4 .... when a man came up and said 'Hand over your

money,' ....

5 I was walking through a field with my dog ....

....

6 .... when some friends called round, ...

....

B Subject and object questions

Look at the facts, and write questions for the answers given in brackets.

Example: Edmund Hillary and Tenzing Norgay climbed Mount Everest in 1953.

Who climbed Mount Everest in 1953?   (Edmund Hillary and Tenzing Norgay)
What did Edmund Hillary and Tenzing Norgay do in 1953?   (They climbed Mount Everest)
When did Edmund Hillary and Tenzing Norgay climb Mount Everest?   (In 1953)

1 In 1972, Mark Spitz won seven Olympic gold medals.

   .... (Mark Spitz)
   .... (Seven)

2 Elizabeth Taylor married Richard Burton twice.

   .... (Elizabeth Taylor)
   .... (Twice)

3 The Americans landed on the moon on 20 July 1969.

   .... (On 20 July 1969)
   .... (The Americans landed on the moon)

C When did it happen?

Think about a time when
- you met a friend for the first time
- you met someone famous
- you went abroad
- you won a prize
- you lost (or found) something valuable
- you got (or nearly got) into serious trouble.

Choose two of the topics and write about them. Say what happened and when it happened.

Time expressions

during the summer holidays
when I was 18
before I went to college
while I was at college
after I left college

1 ....
....
....
....

2 ....
....
....
....

D Active or passive?

Fill the gaps with the correct Past forms of verbs in the box. Choose between active and passive.

hit	steal	release	meet
offer	rob	catch	arrest
escape	chase	begin	kill

Past simple passive

was/were + past participle

Someone killed him → He **was killed**
We caught them → They **were caught**
I wrote it → It **was written**

Clyde Barrow's life of crime .... in December 1926, when he .... some Christmas turkeys from a farm. He .... by the police, but he .... soon afterwards, because he was only 16 years old.

He .... Bonnie Parker in 1930. Together they .... a large number of shops and banks. Innocent people (often) .... in these robberies.

Large rewards .... for their capture, and they .... from State to State by hundreds of police, but they (always) ....

Eventually, in 1934, Bonnie and Clyde .... in a police ambush. Their car .... by a hail of bullets, and they ....

Bonnie and Clyde

TRANSLATION

Translate into your own language:

1 I met them during the summer, while I was travelling through France.

....
....

2 – He was on the phone when I arrived.
– Who was he talking to?
– I don't know. He didn't tell me.

....
....
....

3 The building was damaged in the earthquake, but everyone was rescued.

....
....

Now cover up the left-hand side, and translate your sentences back into English.

LISTENING: Childhood memories

1 You will hear two people describing childhood memories. They are about

   1 going to boarding school
   2 seeing snow for the first time.

   Before you listen, guess which of these sentences appear in each description. Mark them *1* or *2*.

   a I had to be very brave.
   b I can remember having mittens on strings.
   c It was in the mountains.
   d I remember being with my mother and father in the car.
   e It was a very new kind of experience.
   f In fact, I had a lovely time.

   mittens

   ▭ Now listen and check your answers.

2 ▭ Listen again and fill the gaps.

   1 When she was .... old, she was sent to .... She felt .... because she thought she would never .... again. She wanted to .... but she couldn't because her sister was ....

   2 When she was ...., she saw .... for the first time. Her mittens ...., her nose felt .... and her .... were stinging. She remembers the .... and the ....

PRONUNCIATION: Reduced and full forms

1 ▭ Listen to the words underlined in these sentences. Usually, they have the sound /ə/, but they have a full vowel sound when they come at the end of a sentence.

a	Is it for you?	Who's it for?
b	Is he from Australia?	Where's he from?
c	I want to see it.	Do you really want to?
d	I've bought some bread.	Can I have some?
e	He was in the army.	I know who that was.
f	Do you like dancing?	Yes, I do.

2 Choose underlined words from the box to complete these sentences. Mark those that have the sound /ə/.

   a Would you like .... coffee?
   b Where are you going ....?
   c What are you waiting ....?
   d We've run out of sugar. Could you buy ....?
   e She .... carrying an umbrella.
   f Were you afraid? Yes, I ....
   g Where .... they go every evening?

   ▭ Now listen and practise saying the sentences.

20   Unit 3 Past events

READING: Two terrible tales

1 Put the sentences in these stories in the right order.
2 How do you think each story ends? Make a guess, then read the endings at the bottom of the page.

Holiday in New York

1 ...E....   2 ....   3 ....   4 ....   5 ....   6 ....   7 ....   8 ....

A As soon as the doors opened, they rushed out of the lift, and spent a sleepless night in their room.

B At first, they were a bit nervous about being out alone at night, after hearing stories about people being mugged, but they felt safe in the car, and were feeling quite relaxed as they drove back to their hotel.

C The lift came, and the couple jumped in, but the large man started running and got in beside them just as the doors closed.

D The next morning, they decided to fly home, and went down to the reception to check out.

E A British couple were on holiday in New York.

F Immediately, he shouted 'Hit the floor, lady!', and the terrified couple threw themselves down on the floor, throwing all their money and credit cards out of their pockets, and shut their eyes.

G They parked in the basement car park, and were waiting for the lift up to the hotel reception when a large man with a Rottweiler dog appeared out of the shadows and came towards them.

H The first night they hired a car and went to a show on Broadway, followed by an Italian meal.

The bed by the window

1 ...F....   2 ....   3 ....   4 ....   5 ....   6 ....   7 ....   8 ....   9 ....

A He told him about the traffic going by, the children playing in the park opposite, and the birds flying in the trees.

B Sure enough, the next morning, the nurse found the man dead in his bed by the window.

C But his friend, imagining an empty bed over by the window, did nothing – he just closed his eyes and went back to sleep.

D Both men were very old and very ill, and they spent 24 hours a day in bed in the room.

E Fortunately, one of the old men had his bed by the window, and every day he spent hours telling his friend on the other side of the room what he could see through the window.

F Two old men shared a room on the fourth floor of an old people's home in the city centre.

G How nice it would be, he thought, if he had the bed by the window and could see everything for himself, instead of just hearing about it.

H One night, the man by the window called to his friend, 'Quick! Pull the alarm by your bed – I don't think I'm going to last the night!'

I The old man on the inside wall got a lot of pleasure from hearing about the world outside, but after a time he began to get rather jealous.

Holiday in New York: Ending

The receptionist gave them an envelope. Inside were their credit cards and money, and a note which said 'Sorry if I frightened you last night. By the way, "Lady" is the name of my dog.'

The bed by the window: Ending

The old man was very excited as they moved him into the empty bed by the window. He sat up in bed, pulled back the curtain, looked out – and saw a blank brick wall.

4 Money

A Using money

Fill in the missing sentences in these conversations, using one item from Box A and one from Box B.

1 **At a hotel**
   A *I'd like to pay my bill, please.*
   B Certainly. That's $340 altogether.
   A ....
   B Yes, sir. What have you got? Visa? Mastercard?

2 **In a shop**
   A ....
   B They're £4 each.
   A ....
   B Right. That's £8 altogether ... Thank you.
   A ....
   B Yes, of course. I'll just write one out for you.

3 **At an exchange office**
   A ....
   B Yes. If I could just see your passport ... Thanks.
   A ....
   B Just there. Where it says 'signature'.

4 **In the street**
   A Excuse me. ....
   B No, I'm sorry. I can't.
   A ....
   B Yes – there's one just round the corner.

A
Could you give me change ...
Could I have ...
Do you accept ...
How much ...
~~I'd like to pay ...~~
Is there ...
Where do I ...
Can I cash ...
I'll have ...

B
... some traveller's cheques, please
... do these ties cost
~~... my bill please~~
... a receipt, please
... these two, please
... sign them
... credit cards
... for this £10 note
... a bank near here

B The (6) of living

Write the missing words in the diagram. All the answers go across except for number 10, which goes down.

They say that people's standard of living is going up all the time. Well I don't know about the standard of living, but the (6) of living is certainly going up.

Before I even see my salary, the Government takes about 30% of it away in income (2). Then I have to pay the (1) for the apartment, which the landlord's just put up again. And on top of that there are all the (7) for heating, phone and electricity.

It's no better at the shops, either. The (3) of food is unbelievably high these days.

I used to be able to (8) money, but last year I had to close my savings account, because there was no money left in it. And it's getting worse: last month I (4) my whole salary in just one week, and I had to ask my (5) manager for a loan to last me till the end of the month.

It's enough to make you want to jump in front of a train. Only I haven't got any (9) insurance. I can't afford it – it's too (10).

22 Unit 4 Money

C Similar meanings

Rewrite each sentence using a form of the word in brackets, so that they have similar meanings.

Example:
It's expensive. (*cost*)
It costs a lot.

1 It's too expensive for me. (*afford*)
....

2 It's not worth buying. (*waste*)
....

3 It's cheap. (*cost*)
....

4 Can I borrow £5 from you? (*lend*)
....

5 He's borrowed more than $1,000 from his parents. (*owe*)
....

6 They pay him £800 a week. (*earn*)
....

7 He bought that jacket for $500. (*pay*)
....

New words

Use this space to write down new words from the unit, with your own notes and examples.

Unit 4 Money

TRANSLATION

Translate into your own language:

1 I'd like to buy a new video recorder, but I can't afford it.

2 Can you lend me $10? I'll pay you back at the weekend.

3 – Do you think the Government should increase income tax?
– No. I think they should reduce it.

Now cover up the left-hand side, and translate your sentences back into English.

LISTENING: A waste of money

1 You will hear two people talking about things they think are a waste of money. Before you listen, check that you know what these words and phrases mean:

a status symbol   extravagant
to show off   perfume
a treat   dressing table
                   ostentation

2 Listen to the recording. What do you think the *main point* of their argument is?

 a Expensive cars, meals and perfume are a waste of money.
 b It's a waste of money to buy expensive things just to show you can afford them.
 c People have to spend more than they can afford.
 d Most people can only afford expensive things on special occasions.

3 The speakers give several examples of extravagance. According to the speakers, why

 a do people go to expensive restaurants?
 b do people buy expensive cars?
 c do men buy women expensive perfume?
 d do women buy expensive perfume?

PHRASAL VERBS: Intransitive verbs (1)

1 Match the phrasal verbs on the left with their opposites on the right.

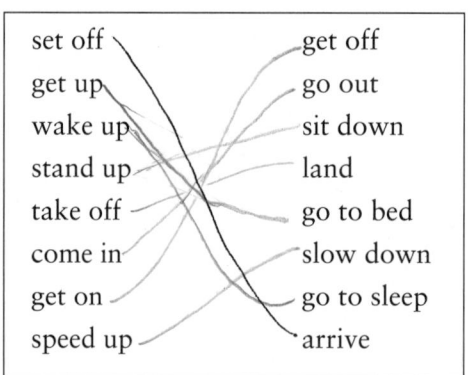

2 The phrasal verbs in these sentences are mixed up. Change them so that they make better sense.

 a Fasten your seat belt. The plane's going to *slow down* soon.   land
 b It's time to *get off* and have some breakfast.   get up
 c I *came in* this morning with a sore throat.   arrived
 d *Wake up*, everybody! The President's here.   wake up / stand up
 e I knocked on the door. '*Stand up*,' said a voice.   come in
 f He put on his rucksack and *got up* towards the mountains.   set off = starten
 g This is my stop. I'm *taking off* here. Goodbye!   getting off
 h She *set off* next to me and took my hand in hers.   set down
 i You'd better *sit down* or you might skid. *
        slow down

See also the Phrasal verbs reference section on the last page of the book.

* schleudern

WRITING SKILLS: Reference: pronouns

1 **Look at the examples.**
   What do the words in *italic type* refer to?

   a – Our coats are in the next room. *Mine*'s a
         brown *one* and *hers* is a black *one*.
       – Is this one *yours*?
       – No, that's *Peter's*.

   b – I need a baby's cot for the weekend. Have
         you got *one*?
       – Yes, of course. You can borrow *ours*.

   c – I left my money at home. Could you lend
         me *some*?
       – Sorry. I haven't got *any* either.

   d My grandfather grows tulips, and his garden
      is full of them – he's got red *ones*, yellow
      ones, pink *ones*, even purple *ones*. *The ones*
      I like best are the white *ones*.

   Mine   = my coat
   one   = ...
   hers   = ...
   yours = ...
   Peter's = ...

   one   = ...
   ours   = ...

   some   = ...
   any   = ...

   ones   = ...
   The ones = ...

2 **Each of these sentences has got one mistake. Correct them.**

   a You can take that book – it's your.
   b If you need a car for the weekend, you can borrow my one.
   c These jeans are too small. Have you got any bigger?
   d Do you want a large coffee or a small?
   e I wanted to get unleaded petrol, but the garage hadn't got some.

3 **Rewrite this story so that the words *soup*, *spoon*, *bread* and *coat* only occur once each. Use words from the box.**

   | it | some | mine |
   | one | any | yours |

   I sat down and waited. Eventually a waiter appeared and I ordered onion soup. After a long time, he brought me some onion soup, and then I noticed that my spoon was dirty. I asked for another spoon. After another long wait, he brought me a clean spoon, but the spoon was much too small, so I asked if I could have a bigger spoon. After about ten minutes, he brought me a spoon that was clean and the right size. Then I noticed that there wasn't any bread, so I called the waiter again and asked him for some bread. He told me there wasn't any bread.
   I finished, paid the bill and asked for my coat. The waiter brought a coat that I didn't recognise at all. I told him it wasn't my coat, and that my coat was a black leather coat. He came back with a brown jacket.
   'Is this your coat?' he asked.

Unit 4 Money

5 Obligation

A Obligation structures

Fill each gap with a suitable form of an expression from the box.

> - have to
> - need to
> - don't have to
> - don't need to
> - can
> - are allowed to
> - can't
> - aren't allowed to

1 There's plenty of time. We ...*have to*... leave yet.
2 – ...*Don't I have to*... (I) wear a tie?
 – No. In fact, you ...*don't*... wear jeans, if you like.
3 If you're a learner driver, you ...*aren't allowed to*... drive on your own. If you want to drive on your own, you ...*need to*... pass your driving test.
4 It's quite strict here. You ...*have to*... be in by midnight, and you ...*don't need to*... have guests in your room.
5 When you come back from abroad, you ...*are allowed to*... bring in 200 duty-free cigarettes and a litre of duty-free spirits.
6 – How long ...*can*... (I) keep these books?
 – For two weeks. If you bring them back later than that, you ...*need to*... pay a fine.

B Make and let

Here's someone talking about his life in the army. Write about him using *make* and *let*.

1. We have to run six kilometres a day.
2. We're allowed to go home one weekend a month.
3. We have to get up at 5.30 in the morning.
4. We're not allowed to have long hair.
5. We don't have to wear uniform on our days off.
6. We're not allowed to complain about the food.

3 They make him get up at 5.30 in the morning.
1 They make him run six km a day
2 They let him go home one weekend a month
4 They let him not to have long hair
5 They let him not wear uniform on the days off
6 They let him not complain about the food

Now imagine four other things that they (don't) make and (don't) let him do.
They make *him polish his boots*
They don't make *him do his own washing*
They let *him drink coca cola*
They don't let *him drive a Jeep*

26 Unit 5 Obligation

C Past and present obligations

How is your life different from when you were a child?
Write about four differences. Use ideas from the box to help you.

going out	going to bed
work	clothes
watching TV	food and drink
friends	play

Examples:

When I was a child ... *go to the cinema*   Now ...
My parents didn't let me drink coffee.   *I can drink as much coffee as I like.*
I didn't have to worry about money.   *I have to earn a living.*

When I was a child ...   Now ...

D Utopia

Imagine an ideal world, in which everything's exactly the way you want it, and you can do whatever you like. Choose two of the following and say a few things about each.

- an ideal job   – an ideal holiday
- an ideal shop   – an ideal school
- an ideal car   – an ideal home life
- ideal parents   – an ideal government

Example: an ideal shop

You can get anything you like. You don't have to pay for anything. It's open 24 hours a day. They deliver everything to your home.

1

2

TRANSLATION

Translate into your own language:

1 You don't have to come if you don't want to.

2 – What qualifications do you need for the job?
– You have to have a university degree.

3 – How many books can I borrow?
– As many as you like.

Now cover up the left-hand side, and translate your sentences back into English.

LISTENING: School rules

You will hear three people talking about the schools they attended.

1 Look at these questions, then listen to the recording. Who answers each question, and what answer do they give? (Write *1, 2* or *3*, and *Yes* or *No*.) Are there any questions that no-one answers?

   a Were the teachers strict in class?
   b Did you have to attend all the classes?
   c Did you have to attend morning prayers?
   d Was sport compulsory?
   e Did you have to do a lot of homework?
   f Were you allowed to leave the school at lunchtime?
   g Could you stay in the classrooms during lunchtime?

2 All three speakers talk about school uniform. Which of these sentences is closest to what each speaker says? (Write *1, 2* or *3*.)

   a Most pupils thought the skirts were too long.
   b The rules about the uniform were too strict.
   c School uniform is quite a good idea.

PRONUNCIATION: Contracted forms

1 Listen to the contracted forms underlined in these sentences.

   She'll see you tomorrow.
   He'd look better with short hair.
   You're making too much noise.
   I haven't seen him.
   They'd met before.
   It isn't working.
   We've seen that film already.

   What are the *full* forms of these words?

2 Look at these sentences. Circle the words you think will be contracted when they are spoken.

   a I do not have any change, I am afraid.
   b They are sure they have not seen him.
   c He will come if he is not busy.
   d I have been to Athens but he has not.
   e You had better look where you are going.
   f I cannot hear the music – it is too quiet.

   Listen to check your answers. Then practise saying the sentences.

READING: Three word games

Each of these games can be played by a group of several players. After each game there are some questions. The answers are given at the bottom of the page.

1 First and last

First of all, the players choose a category, such as People's First Names, Countries, Household Objects, TV Programmes, Things to Eat & Drink, Animals.

Let's say the category is Animals. The first player calls out any word that belongs to the category (e.g. *cat*). Then each player in turn has to think of another word, beginning with the last letter of the previous word. So after *cat*, the second player might call out *tiger*, followed by *rhinoceros, sheep, pony, yak, koala bear*, and so on. All the words must belong to the category, and you're not allowed to use any word twice.

If a player can't think of a word, calls out the wrong kind of word, or repeats a word, he/she is out of the game. The winner is the last player left in the game.

TEST YOURSELF

It's your turn. What word do you call out?

a Dresden, New York, Kabul, Lima, Amsterdam …
b India, Afghanistan, Norway, Yemen …
c Chips, spaghetti, ice-cream, meat, tomato …

2 Rhyme and mime

One player thinks of a word (e.g. *ghost*) and writes it down, and tells the other players a word that rhymes with it (e.g. *most*). The other players have to guess the word you have written down.

The difficult bit is that you *are not allowed to speak*. Instead, you must *mime* your guess. So if you think the answer might be *toast*, you could act out putting some bread in a toaster, taking it out, and spreading some jam on it. The winning player, in this case, will be the one pretending to be a ghost.

TEST YOURSELF

What words do you think these people are miming?

a rhymes with *seller*   c rhymes with *tight*

b rhymes with *go*   d rhymes with *said*

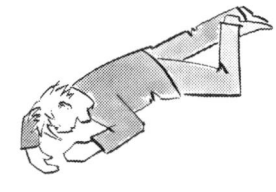

3 Letter by letter

The aim of the game is to build up a word letter by letter – but not to complete a word yourself.

To start, one player calls out a letter. Player 2 adds a letter, Player 3 adds another, and so on round the circle. There are two rules about adding letters:
– you must have a real (longer) word in mind.
– once you get past the third letter, you mustn't add a letter that completes a word.

Here's an example with four players:

Player 1: B
Player 2: E   (= BE. Words with fewer than four letters don't count.)
Player 3: L   (= BEL)
Player 4: O   (= BELO. Danger! Will Player 1 have to complete the word BELOW?)
Player 1: N   (= BELON. Bad luck, Player 2!)
Player 2: G   (The only possibility.)

If it's your turn, and you can't think what word the previous player has in mind, you can challenge the player (e.g. if Player 2 adds E instead of G, making BELONE, Player 3 should challenge). If the challenged player can't tell you a sensible word, he/she loses. Otherwise, you lose!

It's best if each player starts with three lives. Each time a player has to finish a word, he/she loses one life. Players who have lost three lives are out of the game. The winner is the last player left at the end.

TEST YOURSELF

What do you do in these situations? The letters so far are

a H – A – P – P –
b R – E – F – U – S –
c J – U – S – H –

Answers

First and last
Some possibilities:
a Montreal, Madrid, Moscow, Madras, Montevideo
b Nigeria, Nepal (*not Norway* – no repeats!)
c orange, okra, onion, omelette

Rhyme and mime
a umbrella
b throw
c fight
d dead

Letter by letter
a E (for *happen*) or I (for *happily* or *happiness*). *Not Y!*
b A (for *refusal*) or I (for *refusing*). *Not E!*
c Challenge the previous player. He/she is trying to trick you!

6 On holiday

A Holiday activities

Imagine what these people did on their holidays. Use the words in the box to help you, and add ideas of your own.

We went on a walking holiday in the Scottish Highlands. ....

We went on a coach tour through Italy. ....

We went on a seaside package holiday to Florida. ....

| art gallery |
| backpack |
| camp |
| climb |
| cook |
| excursion |
| hotel |
| museum |
| sightseeing |
| souvenir |
| speciality |
| tent |
| visit |
| waterski |

B Holiday puzzle

The square contains 25 hidden words. Words can run in any direction: forward, backward, up, down, and diagonally. See if you can find:

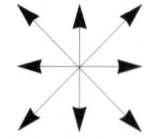

1 five ways of getting to your holiday destination
  B *oat* T *rain* C   B   P

2 two kinds of holiday
  P   C

3 two documents you might need to go on holiday
  P   T

4 two places to go sightseeing
  C   C

5 two things to wear on a summer holiday
  S   S

6 somewhere to spend the day on a summer holiday
  B

7 three things to do at the seaside
  S   W   S

8 two things to do on a winter holiday
  S   S

9 two ways of eating in the open air
  P   B

10 two things you may need on a walking holiday
  C   M

11 two things to help you remember your holiday
  S   C

S	B	E	N	A	L	P	F	A	B	E
T	O	C	A	M	E	R	A	D	U	X
E	A	R	I	N	E	V	U	O	S	T
K	T	W	I	N	D	S	U	R	F	S
C	S	A	P	A	C	K	A	G	E	S
I	R	W	K	S	A	I	L	N	H	A
T	R	O	P	S	S	A	P	I	C	P
O	S	H	O	R	T	S	C	P	A	M
S	A	N	D	A	L	S	H	M	E	O
E	N	E	U	C	E	B	R	A	B	C
L	A	R	D	E	H	T	A	C	J	Y

30   Unit 6 On holiday

C Festival

Write about a festival or other traditional celebration in your country.
Use these questions to help you decide what to say.

- What's the festival called?
- What time of year does it take place?
- What does it celebrate?
- How long does it last?
- Do people wear special costumes?
- Do people eat special food?
- Are there any parades?
- What other activities take place?

....
....
....
....
....
....
....
....

New words

Use this space to write down new words from the unit, with your own notes and examples.

TRANSLATION

Translate into your own language:

1 We went on an excursion to the Alhambra on Saturday.

2 If you want to buy some souvenirs, try the local market – the carpets are really good value for money.

3 The Festival takes place in late August, and lasts for three weeks.

Now cover up the left-hand side, and translate your sentences back into English.

LISTENING: Going home

You will hear a travel courier describing something that happened at the end of a holiday. The story is in two parts.

1 Here are some events from Part 1 of the story. Try to guess what order they are in.

  a ☐ They checked in for their flights.
  b ☐ They started complaining.
  c ☐ We took everyone to the airport.
  d ☐ He put his hands round my throat.
  e ☐ Five men were going to Manchester.
  f ☐ One of the men started shouting.
  g ☐ Their flight was over-booked.
  h ☐ I found them a flight for the next afternoon.

  Now listen to Part 1 and check your answers.

2 Here are some words and phrases from Part 2 of the story.

  … security guards …   … released …
  … guns …   … London …
  … calm things down …   … new job …
  … arrested …

  Listen and make complete sentences, to give an outline of Part 2.

PHRASAL VERBS: Intransitive verbs (2)

1 Look at these phrasal verbs. Listen to the examples and note down what you think the verbs mean, in English or your own language. Use a dictionary to check.

carry on	find out	get on
grow up	turn up	settle down
set off		

2 Read this text, and replace the words in italics with phrasal verbs from the box.

   I recently read my grandfather's diaries, and I *(a) learned* a lot of interesting things about his life. Apparently he *(b) spent his childhood* in California. He and his parents *(c) didn't like being together* at all, and when he was 18 he decided to see America. He *(d) started on his journey* with very little money and travelled east. He *(e) continued* until he reached Detroit, where he got a job washing up in a restaurant. He fell in love with one of the waitresses, and one day he *(f) appeared* at her flat with a bunch of roses and asked her to marry him. Surprisingly, she agreed, and he *(g) went to live* with her in Detroit, where they had 10 children.

   a ....   e ....
   b ....   f ....
   c ....   g ....
   d ....

See also the Phrasal verbs reference section on the last page of the book.

WRITING SKILLS: Subject and object relative clauses

1 Here are some photos taken by a foreign student in Cambridge.

These people lived next door.

This cathedral was built in the 11th century.

I met this girl at a party.

We visited this place on an excursion.

I stayed with this family.

I studied at this school.

He could also talk about them using relative clauses:

This is a photo of …

… the people *who* lived next door.
… a cathedral *which* was built in the 11th century.
… a girl (*who*) I met at a party.
… a place (*which*) we visited on an excursion.
… the family (*who*) I stayed with.
… the school (*which*) I studied at.

The first two examples are *subject* **relative clauses. Instead of** *who* **or** *which*, **we can use** *that*:
– This is a photo of the people *that* lived next door.

The other examples are *object* **relative clauses. Instead of** *who* **or** *which*, **we can use** *that* **or nothing:**
– This is a photo of | a girl *that* I met at a party.
                     | a girl I met at a party.

2 Fill the gaps in this letter with the relative clauses in Part 1.

I had quite a good time in Cambridge, although .... was rather boring – they spent a lot of time watching TV and didn't go out much. Fortunately, ... were very friendly, so I spent a lot of time with them. Also, ... organised trips at the weekends, so I went to quite a lot of interesting places. I'm sending you some photos of .... It's just a small town but it's got .... The person in the foreground is .... – her name's Véronique.

3 These sentences describe other photos the student took. Change them so they begin *This is a photo of …*

a These students were in my class.

....

b I could see this building from my bedroom window.

....

c This person taught us English.

....

d We organised this party at the end of term.

....

e I came home on this train.

....

Review: Units 1–6

1 Sentence rewriting

Rewrite these sentences using the words given.

Example:
They deliver 300 million letters every day.
300 million letters *are delivered every day.*

1 He goes abroad four times a year.
   He goes abroad every three months.
2 My brother always washes the dishes.
   My brother always is washing up.
3 I met them while I was on my summer holiday.
   I met them during *my summer holiday.*
4 Mario Puzo wrote *The Godfather*.
   The Godfather was written by Mario Puzo.
5 Could I borrow your car?
   Would you lend *me your car* ?
6 We have to go to bed early.
   .... allowed ....
7 They didn't let me go out.
   They made *me not going out.*

2 Asking questions

Complete the questions.

Example:
– Where *do you work*?
– At Barclays Bank in the High Street. I'm a secretary.

1 – *How often do you* eat out?
   – About once a week, if I can afford it.
2 – How *many children have you got*
   – Three. Two girls and a boy.
3 – What *weather was during your holiday*
   – It was cold, but quite sunny.
4 – *What was he doing* when you arrived?
   – He was packing a suitcase.
5 – Do you like my jacket? I got it for my birthday.
   – Really? Who *gave it to you* ?
6 – *Could you change* this £5 note?
   – No, I'm sorry. I haven't got any change.
7 – .... a suit?
   – No. You can wear whatever you like.

3 Vocabulary

1 Match the types of person with the activities.
   culture-vulture   doing overtime
   outdoor type   going to parties
   sociable type   visiting art galleries
   workaholic   going for walks

2 What machine or tool would you use to
   a make a hole? ....
   b keep things cool? ....
   c clean the floor? ....
   d wash clothes? ....

3 Match the items on the left with those on the right.
   riot   people drown
   earthquake   people are arrested
   war   the ground shakes
   flood   cities are shelled

4 Complete these sentences.
   a The .... for my flat is going up again.
   b People with jobs have to pay income ....
   c We pay our electricity .... every two months.
   d If you've got a family, it's a good idea to take out some life ...., in case you die.

5 Match the items on the left with those on the right.
   souvenirs   restaurants
   local specialities water
   excursions   buses
   windsurfing   fine buildings
   sightseeing   shops

34 Review Units 1–6

4 Fill the gaps

Fill each gap with *one* suitable word. Example:

I ....*was*.... walking through the park yesterday when I suddenly ....*heard*.... a loud scream. *brüllen, schreien*

1 My flatmate is a very difficult person to live with. *Mitbewohner* He ....*leaves*.... his things lying all over the place – he never ....*puts*.... anything away. His room's always in a terrible ....*mess*.... . He wastes electricity, too. He always forgets to switch the light ....*off*.... when he goes out of the room, and when he washes up (which isn't very often) he leaves the hot ....*water*.... running and uses ....*mostly*.... all the hot water.

2 Fresh fruit is very good ....*value*.... for money. It's cheap and it's good for you. Caviare, on the other hand, is a complete ....*waste*.... of money. It's ridiculously expensive – most people can't *lächerlich* ....*afford*.... to buy it.

3 The teachers at our school are really easy-going. They don't make us wear a school ....*uniform*.... we can wear ....*anything*.... we like. And we ....*never*.... have to do homework if we don't want to. They even ....*let*.... us smoke in the playground.

5 Writing paragraphs

Write a short paragraph (2 or 3 sentences) on the following:

1 What's going on in your life at the moment? Are you busy? How are you spending your time?

....
....
....

2 Imagine a room where you could really relax. What's it like?

....
....
....

3 Write about a frightening experience you had. What were you doing at the time? What happened next?

....
....
....

4 Think of a festival or celebration in your country. When does it happen? What do people do?

....
....
....

6 Dictation

You will hear someone talking about two holidays which went badly wrong.

Listen and write down what you hear.

7 Past and present

A Used to

Rewrite these sentences using *used to*.

Forms of *used to*
They **used to** live in Australia.
There **used to** be a bank near here.
I **didn't use to** like Chinese food.
Did your parents **use to** read you bedtime stories?

1 We *worked* long hours, but we *didn't get* much pay.
   We used to work long hours, but we didn't use to get much pay.

2 There *was* a cinema near my house. I *went* there every Saturday.
   There used to be a cinema near my house. I used to go there every Saturday.

3 – How *did* you *get* to school?
   – I *walked*. And when I was older, I *cycled*.
   How did you use to get to school?
   I used to walk. And when I was older I used to cycle.

4 There *wasn't* much traffic in those days. We *played* football in the street.
   There didn't use to be much traffic in those days. We used to play football ....

B THINGS HAVE CHANGED

All the verbs in these paragraphs are in the Present perfect tense.
Fill the gaps with the past participle of verbs from the box.

I've **STOPPED** smoking, I've **THROWN** my TV in the dustbin, I've **JOINED** a fitness club, I've **LEARNED** how to swim, I've **GIVEN** up eating chips, and I've already **LOST** five kilos.

He's **BOUGHT** a new suit, he's **HAD** a haircut, he's **SHAVED** off his beard and he's **APPLIED** for a job.

She's **CLOSED** her bank account, she's **TAUGHT** herself Spanish, she's **PAID** all her bills, she's **RESIGNED** from her job, she's **CHANGED** her name, she's **GONE** to Mexico, she's **STARTED** a new life.

apply
buy
change
close
give
go
have
join
learn
lose
pay
resign
shave
start
stop
teach
throw

If your answers are right, the letters in circles will spell out the name of the exercise.

C How have they changed?

The pictures show three people as they were ten years ago, and as they are now.
Imagine how their lives have changed. Write a few sentences about each one.

She used to be a famous rock star. She's spent all her money. People don't ask her for her autograph any more. They don't buy her records any more.

D Present perfect passive

What's happened to the things in the pictures?
Complete the sentences using verbs from the box.
Use the Present perfect passive.

Present perfect passive

has/have been + past participle

Someone's killed him → He's been killed
We've caught them → They've been caught
I've repaired it → It's been repaired

break	feed	polish
cancel	mend	tear
cut down	open	wash

1 The trees *have been cut down.*
2 The clothes ....
3 The candlestick ....
4 The cup ....
5 The concert ....
6 The letters ....
7 The cat ....

Unit 7 Past and present   37

TRANSLATION

Translate into your own language:

1 I used to go sailing nearly every weekend, but I've given it up now.

Früher ging ich fast jedes Wochenende segeln, aber ich habe es jetzt aufgegeben.

2 The cinema's been pulled down, and the theatre's been turned into a supermarket.

Das Kino ist abgerissen worden und das Theater wurde e. Supermarkt umgebaut

3 He doesn't live with his parents any longer. He's moved into a flat.

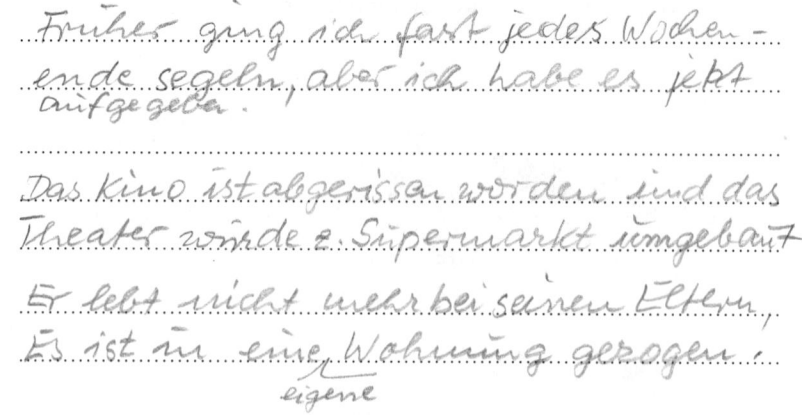

Er lebt nicht mehr bei seinen Eltern. Er ist in eine Wohnung gezogen. (eigene)

Now cover up the left-hand side, and translate your sentences back into English.

LISTENING: Changed lives

1 🔊 You will hear three people talking about how their lives have changed. Listen and complete these sentences.

Speaker 1: She used to be a *sales representitiv* ~~uly~~, but now she's become a *promotion*.

Speaker 2: He used to be *single*, but now he's *married* and has *small baby*.

Speaker 3: She used to work as a *production assistent* in a *T.V. company* but she's *changed* and now she works for a *national charity*.

2 Which speakers are these statements true of?

🔊 Listen again and write 1, 2 and/or 3 in the table.

He/She …

a *1,3* used to travel more.	
b *1,2* spends more time at home now.	
c *1* has more money now.	
d *1,2* has more responsibility now.	
e *3* has an easier life now.	
f *1,2,3* is happier now.	

PRONUNCIATION: Syllables and stress

1 These words have different numbers of syllables:

sport , eve ning , news pa per , A me ri ca

How many syllables are there in these words?

murder	photograph	magazine	understand
murdered	cars	library	religious
murderer	published	picked	international

🔊 Listen to the recording to check.

2 Notice that some words have only one stress:

murder, religious, library, America

Other words have two stresses, a main stress and a secondary stress:

understand, international, magazine, photograph

🔊 Listen to the recording.

3 Look at these sentences. Find words with more than two syllables. Mark the main stress in each, and also the secondary stress if there is one.

a She's studying architecture at London University.
b They interviewed the new President on television.
c Here's another photograph of my grandparents.
d He works as a journalist for a local newspaper.
e I don't understand this – it's too complicated.

🔊 Now listen and practise saying the sentences.

38 Unit 7 Past and present

READING: Two childhoods

In these extracts from an interview, a father remembers what life was like when he was seven years old, and describes the lifestyle of his own seven-year-old son.

Paul in 1956, aged 7

My father died when I was a baby, and my mother went out to work. I was an only child, so I had no brothers or sisters to play with …

… I used to play in the street with other children, or ride my bike down to the park, but I remember I spent a lot of time just sitting at home reading. We had a television, I think, but I don't remember watching it very much …

… My grandparents lived with us and we used to do a lot of things together – I remember we played cards a lot. At the weekends, my mother always used to take me out – we often went down to the sea and swam, and I learned to swim when I was quite young …

… We didn't have a car, so we went everywhere by bus. Occasionally, one of my uncles used to come and take us out in his car, which was a great treat. For holidays we always went to the seaside, but never very far away – maybe a short train journey …

… My mother wasn't very strict with me, and I don't remember her ever hitting me. In fact, I used to get my own way too much, and I had a pretty fiery temper. So sometimes she made me go up to my bedroom until I'd calmed down …

… I was given pocket money, a small amount because we weren't very rich, and I probably spent most of it on sweets, as far as I remember – I don't think anyone thought they were bad for you then.

Jack in 1994, aged 7

We've got two children: Jack is seven, and his little brother Ed is four. They're quite close, and play a lot together. They fight quite a lot too, but on the whole they enjoy each other's company …

… Unfortunately, we live quite a long way away from the rest of the family. It's an eight-hour drive to get to their grandparents, but we usually visit them during the school holidays …

… Jack reads well, but he hasn't started to read for pleasure yet – he thinks reading is only something you have to do at school. I think the main problem is that he watches far too much television …

… Apart from TV, he likes playing cards and computer games. And riding his bike. I don't let him ride it on the streets, but we often go to the park, where it's safer …

… He's quite sensible about sweets, because he's getting his adult teeth now, and he knows they've got to last him for life. He seems more interested in saving his pocket money and counting it than spending it …

… He can be difficult sometimes. He likes to have his own way, but then so do I, so we do have arguments. Occasionally, I'll smack his bottom, but only as a last resort …

… We go to the local swimming pool about once a week, but during the summer we usually fly off somewhere warm where we can swim in the sea.

Which seven-year-old would you expect to say these things? Write P, J, PJ (for both) or ✘ (for neither).

a ………… My brother's not too bad really.
b ………… I never get smacked.
c ………… But *why* can't I go to the park on my own?
d ………… I wish Grandma lived nearer.
e ………… I've got a bike.
f ………… I wish we had a television.
g ………… Are we *really* going out in a *car*?

h ………… I think reading's really boring.
i ………… I hate swimming.
j ………… Shall we have a game of cards?
k ………… I'm saving up for a new video game.
l ………… I'm *not* going to tidy my room!
m ………… I've never been in a plane.
n ………… It's best not to eat too many sweets.

8 At your service

A Having things done

1 What places are shown in the pictures? Write the names underneath each one.

| Electrician's | photographer's | Motormechanic's |

| dry-Cleaner's | dentist's surgery | heardresser's | optician's |

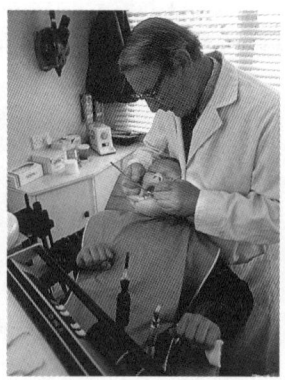

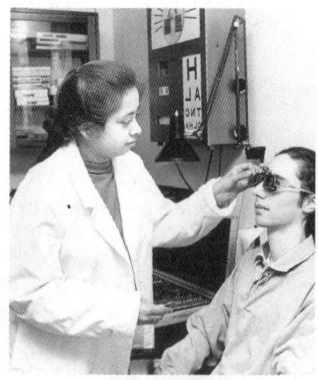

2 Imagine that you went to each of the places last week.
What did you have done at each place? Use verbs from the box.

a *I had my TV repaired (at the electrician's).*
b I had my foto taken at the photographer's
c I had my car repaired at... (mended, serviced)
d I had my clothes cleaned at...
e I had my teeth filled at.... (checked)
f I had my hair cuted at the...
g I had my glases

- d clean
- f cut
- e fill
- mend
- c repair
- service
- b take
- test
- wash

hair: dyed (gefärbt)
      rinsed getönt, gespült
      streaked gesträhnt

future: I'm going to have my photo taken
                          rute treatment Wurzelbehandlg.

my wisdom teeth = Weisheitszähne

B How do you do it?

Fill the gaps in these conversations with words from the box.

> weigh   parcel   registered
> form   coins   receiver
> dial   member   post office
> card   stamps   local area code
> join   borrow   international code

1 **At the library**
   - I'd like to ...*borrow*... these three books, please.
   - Fine. Can I have your membership ...*card*...?
   - Um, I'm afraid I'm not a ...*member*... .
   - Well, you can ...*join*... (beitreten) now if you like. Just fill in this ...*form*... .

2 **Using the phone**
   - How do I use this phone?
   - OK. First lift the ...*receiver*..., and then put some ...*coins*... in the slot. Then you ...*dial*... your number.
   - How about phoning Britain?
   - You ...*dial*... 00 and then 44, which is the ...*international code*... for Britain. Then you dial the ...*local area code*... (without the initial 0), and then the number.

3 **Postal services**
   - I want to send this ...*parcel*... to London. What do I do?
   - Take it to the ...*post office*... and they'll ...*weigh*... it for you. Then you buy the ...*stamps*... and stick them on, and give it to the person behind the counter.
   - Will it get there safely? It's got something quite valuable in it.
   - Then it's better to send it by ...*registered*... post. But that's quite expensive.

New words

Use this space to write down new words from the unit, with your own notes and examples.

Unit 8 At your service

TRANSLATION

Translate into your own language:

1. – Where do you have your hair done?
   – Well actually, I do it myself.

   Wo hast Du Dein Haar machen lassen
   Oh, das habe ich selbst gemacht
   Eigentlich

2. – Can I help you?
   – Yes. I'd like to make an appointment to see the doctor, please.

   Kann ich Dir helfen?
   Ja. Ich möchte gern einen Arzttermin vereinbaren.

3. She picked up the phone and dialled 999. A voice said, 'Do you want the police, fire service or ambulance?'

   Sie hob den Hörer ab und wählte 3x die 9. Eine Stimme sagte: Wollen Sie die Polizei, die Feuerwehr oder die Sanitäter?

Now cover up the left-hand side, and translate your sentences back into English.

LISTENING: On the phone

🎧 You will hear three short telephone conversations. Listen and answer the questions.

1. Complete the notes that the dentist's receptionist made.

   Patient's name: ....
   Problem: ....
   Appointment at: ....

2. Complete the missing information.

   A man phones the .... because he needs a .... They do .... photos together, and it costs .... It takes .... to take the photo and .... to develop it. The shop is open till ....

3. Find *five* differences between this text and the recording.

   A man phones the garage because his Mercedes is making a strange whistling noise. He last had it serviced about a year ago. He arranges to take it into the garage at 8.30 that evening.

PHRASAL VERBS: Transitive verbs (1)

1. Look at these examples:

turn on	Shall I *turn* the radio *on*?
or	Shall I *turn on* the radio?
but	Shall I *turn* it *on*? (not ~~turn on it~~)
ring up	I *rang* my mother *up*.
or	I *rang up* my mother.
but	I *rang* her *up*. (not ~~rang up her~~)

   Notice the position of *on* and *up*. They can come *before* or *after* a noun (*the radio*, *my mother*) but only *after* a pronoun (*it, her*).

2. Look at the the phrasal verbs on the left. Which nouns on the right do you think they go with?

turn up	the TV
switch off	your friends
look up	the tap *Wasserhahn*
throw away	my boots
ring up	these glasses
take off	the light
turn off	your empty bottles
try on	the word 'pronoun'
sort out	our holiday photos

   🎧 Now listen to the recording, and write down each phrasal verb with the noun that goes with it.
   Example: turn up the TV *or* turn the TV up.

   See also the Phrasal verbs reference section on the last page of the book.

WRITING SKILLS: Punctuation: direct speech

1 Look at these examples of direct speech.

'Good evening,' he said. 'My name's Alan.'
'My name's Alan,' he said, 'and this is my sister Rachel.'
He added, 'We used to live in this house.'
'What's your name?' he asked.
He asked me, 'How long have you been here?'
'Help!' he screamed.

Notice how the examples follow these patterns (C = capital letter):

'C... ...,' he said. 'C... ... .'
'C... ...,' he said, 'and ... .'
He said, 'C... ... .'
'C... ...?' he asked.

Note: instead of single quotation marks ('...'), we can use double ones ("...").

Answer these questions.

a Look at the beginning of each bit of direct speech. When do we use a capital letter? When don't we use a capital letter?

b Look at the end of each bit of direct speech. Which comes first: the full stop (.) or the quotation mark (')? What about commas (,)?

2 Correct the mistakes in these sentences.

a 'I'm hungry', he said, 'Is there anything to eat?'

....

b 'Don't go yet,' he begged her. 'stay a little longer'.

....

c He asked me quietly. 'Do you know why I'm here.'

....

d I said, here's the money I owe you.

....

e 'I may be poor', he said, 'But I'm not stupid'

....

3 Add the necessary punctuation to this text.

There was a ring at the door I went to open it and found an old woman standing outside I'm sorry to trouble you sir she said but I'm collecting old clothes to sell have you got anything you can give me wait a minute I told her and went into the bedroom I found an old jumper and a pair of shoes and went back to the front door the woman looked taller and younger than before and she was pointing a gun at me don't move she said or I'll shoot

....

....

....

....

....

....

....

....

Unit 8 At your service

9 Imagining

A Would and wouldn't

Look at the pictures and complete the sentences, saying what you think would/wouldn't happen. Give two continuations for each sentence.

Example: If the chandelier fell down …

… it would break the table.
… they wouldn't be able to finish their meal.
… there would be a terrible mess.
… someone would probably get hurt.

1 If the Loch Ness monster suddenly appeared …
   ....
   ....

2 If someone stole their car …
   ....
   ....

3 If his parents came home …
   ....
   ....

4 If the lion got out …
   ....
   ....

5 If the waiter tripped over …
   ....
   ....

44   Unit 9 Imagining

B Second conditionals

Complete these sentences.

Example: This room would look much better …

… *if you bought a new carpet.*
… *if the walls were a lighter colour.*
… *if it didn't have so much furniture in it.*

> **Second conditionals**
>
> **If + Past tense … would**
> If I **had** enough money, I'd retire.
> You**'d** feel better if you **didn't smoke**.
> If they **doubled** the price of petrol, there **wouldn't be** so much traffic on the roads.

1 He'd look much more attractive ………………………………………………………………………….
2 If I found $100 in the street ……………………………………………………………………………….
3 ……………………………………………………………………… there would be riots in the streets.
4 I wouldn't have to get up so early ………………………………………………………………………….
5 If you really loved me …………………………………………………………………………………………
6 ………………………………………………………………………………………… I'd reduce income tax.
7 I'd be much happier ……………………………………………………………………………………….

C Wishes

What do you think these people might be thinking?
Write two or three wishes for each situation.

> **Expressing wishes**
>
> My head hurts → I wish my head didn't hurt
> I'm lonely → I wish I wasn't lonely
> They're still here → I wish they would go
> I can't swim → I wish I could swim

1 *I wish someone would give us a lift.*
   …………………………………………………………………
   …………………………………………………………………
   …………………………………………………………………
   …………………………………………………………………

2 …………………………………………………………………
   …………………………………………………………………
   …………………………………………………………………
   …………………………………………………………………
   …………………………………………………………………

3 …………………………………………………………………
   …………………………………………………………………
   …………………………………………………………………
   …………………………………………………………………
   …………………………………………………………………

TRANSLATION

Translate into your own language:

1 I wouldn't like to live in Britain. It's too cold and wet.

2 – What would you do if you found some money in the street?
   – I'd hand it in to the police.

3 I wish I didn't have to get up so early in the morning.

....

Now cover up the left-hand side, and translate your sentences back into English.

LISTENING: What would you do?

1 🔊 You will hear two people answering the questions in *Focus on Form* Exercise 1 (Classroom Book, page 45). Listen and complete the table. (Write ✔ or ✘.)

Would you ...	1	2
... give a lift to a hitch-hiker at night?		
... give money to a beggar?		
... cheat in an examination?		
... drive under the influence of alcohol?		
... give up your seat for an elderly person?		
... kill someone in self-defence?		

2 Which speaker do you think would say these remarks? Mark them *1*, *2*, *Both* or *Neither*.

a 'If I were alone in the car, I might pick up a hitch-hiker to keep me company.'
b 'I used to drink and drive when I was younger.'
c 'I never drink alcohol.'
d 'I'd probably give money to a woman begging with a child.'
e 'I think you should respect elderly people.'
f 'I'm not as honest as I'd like to be.'
g 'Killing people is always wrong.'

🔊 Listen again and check your answers.

PRONUNCIATION:
Linking words: consonant + vowel

1 Practise saying these pairs of words. The first ends in a consonant sound, and the second begins with a vowel sound. Try to link the sounds together.

red apple   speak English
wet umbrella   American elections
give up   work abroad
farm animal   thin ice

🔊 Now listen and check.

2 🔊 Listen to these links between /r/ and a vowel sound. Practise saying them.

mother and father   where am I?
the Tower of Babel   they're Italian
after all   four apples

3 Find links between consonant and vowel sounds in these sentences. Draw lines to connect them.

a The books are on the table in the corner.
b It's a waste of money to buy lots of clothes.
c I drink at least a litre of milk every day.
d Wake up and put your clothes on – they've arrived.
e My sister and I are about the same height.
f Small igloos take just over an hour to build.

🔊 Now listen and practise saying the sentences.

READING: My perfect weekend

Here is a regular feature from a magazine: an interview in which someone imagines a perfect weekend.

My perfect weekend
No. 53: Tania Field, photographer

1 Match the questions with their replies.

1 Where would you go?
2 How would you get there?
3 Where would you stay?
4 What, if any, medicines would you take with you?
5 What essential piece of clothing would you take?
6 What would you eat and drink?
7 What would you read?
8 What would you watch on television?
9 Would you play any sport?
10 Who would be your least welcome guest?
11 What three things would you leave behind?
12 What three things would you most like to do?
13 To whom would you send a postcard?
14 What souvenir would you bring home?
15 What would you like to find when you got home?

a A whole pile of detective stories.

b A strict vegetarian; a busload of tourists.

c Lots of everything: fresh squid, octopus, grilled meat, salad, feta cheese, wine and mineral water. In a restaurant right on the beach.

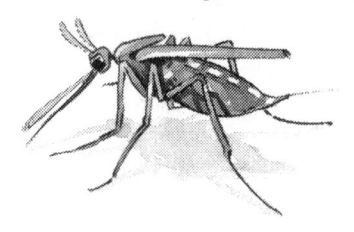

d Play backgammon; buy yesterday's paper after the evening boat comes and read it in a café in the main square; relax.

e For some reason, the restaurants all have TVs, sometimes even outside, so I suppose I'd have to watch whatever everyone else was watching.

f A full fridge; no rain; no phone messages; and someone to meet me at the airport with a car.

g I'd have to have something to kill mosquitoes.

h I'd rent a room in an old house overlooking the harbour, but not the one over the fish shop.

i To a small Greek island whose name I'm not going to tell you. It's hot but green, with olive trees and goats and clear water.

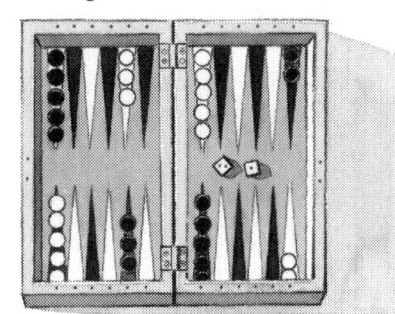

j A large jar of honey. And at least 20 new Greek words.

k A large sunhat.

l I'd swim, especially in the late afternoon, and I'd stroll around, especially in the evening.

m My alarm clock, my word-processor and the phone.

n I'd fly on a plane full of tourists to a large nearby island full of large tourist hotels, and then sail away on the evening boat leaving them all behind.

o No-one. I'd buy a lot, write two or three, and then forget to post them.

2 Find words in the text which describe the five pictures.

3 Are these statements true or false? How do you know?

a Tania Field will get badly sunburnt.
b She's been to the island before.
c She likes mixing with other tourists when she's on holiday.
d She's learning Greek.
e She has a busy life at home.

Unit 9 Imagining 47

10 Describing things

A Identifying objects

1 Match the descriptions with the names and the pictures.

	Name	Picture		Name	Picture
a			f		
b			g		
c			h		
d			i		
e			j		

disk	razor
drill	receipt
map	souvenir
nappy	stapler
plug	typewriter

a A tool that's used to make holes in hard materials.
b Something you buy to remind you of a place you've visited.
c A piece of paper you can use to prove that you've bought something.
d Something you put on babies to keep them dry.
e Something sharp that is used for shaving.
f A drawing that shows you where different places are.
g A small round object that stops the water going out of a basin or bath.
h Something you use to fix a number of pieces of paper together.
i Something you use to store computer programs and word-processing files.
j A machine you use for typing.

2 Now write your own descriptions of

a a hammer ....
....

b a toothbrush ....
....

c a key ....
....

48   Unit 10 Describing things

B Compound nouns

Look at the clues and write the names of the objects in the spaces given. Use a dictionary if necessary. If you're right, the *circled letters* in each answer should be the same.

Three kinds of compound noun

a matchbox = a **box** that you keep **matches** in
running shoes = **shoes** you use for **running**
bottle-opener = something that **opens bottles**

1. This saves you washing up after dinner.
2. This wakes you up in the morning.
3. Wear these on your hands in the car.
4. It gives you a sharp point for writing.
5. It's in a tube in the bathroom.
6. Look in this to see what you want to buy.
7. Juventus players wear these on their feet.
8. Wrap up your presents in this.
9. Wear this when it's raining.
10. Drivers look in this to see behind them.
11. Use this to turn the light on and off.
12. They protect your eyes from the sun.

Now use the circled letters from answers 1–12 to complete this sentence:

Compound nouns

New words

Use this space to write down new words from the unit, with your own notes and examples.

TRANSLATION

Translate into your own language:

1 It's a tool you use to get nails out of wood.

2 – What do you call that liquid you use for washing dishes?
– Washing-up liquid.

3 SECOND-HAND ELECTRIC DRILL FOR SALE. VERY GOOD CONDITION.

Now cover up the left-hand side, and translate your sentences back into English.

LISTENING: Things for sale

1 Look at these small ads for cookers.

> FOR SALE. Electric cooker. 10 years old. Good condition. Single oven. Overhead grill. 889438.
>
> **AEG 'SUPERB' COOKER FOR SALE. Excellent condition. Four burners. Oven with fan. £200 o.n.o. 964235.**
>
> FOR SALE. Gas cooker. Four burners. Large oven. 3 years old. 852368.

🔊 You will hear someone phoning to enquire about a cooker for sale. Write a small ad that exactly fits the description you hear.

2 🔊 You will hear someone phoning to enquire about a desk for sale. Listen and decide which sentences are true and which are false.

a It's an old desk.
b The seller bought it several years ago.
c It's made of solid walnut.
d He won't accept less than £60 for it.
e The buyer will come and see it later today.

Which of these is the desk in the description?

PHRASAL VERBS: Transitive verbs (2)

1 Look at these sentences, and match them with the topics in the box.

1 I can't *work* it *out*.
2 I'll have to *think* it *over*.
3 We'll have to *put* it *off*. *verschiebe*
4 I *made* it *up* myself.
5 I'm trying to *give* it *up*.
6 I *took* it *up* a few weeks ago.
    = start it

| 5 coffee |
| 6 jogging |
| 4 a song |
| 7 a maths problem |
| 2 a suggestion |
| 3 a football match |

🔊 Now listen and check your answers. Then write down the meaning of each phrasal verb in your own language.

2 Replace the words in italics with phrasal verbs.

a I really should *stop eating* chocolate – I'm putting on too much weight. *give up*
b She's *started learning* Spanish again. *took up*
c I'm terrible at paying bills – I always *postpone* it for as long as possible. *put off*
d I looked at the map, but I couldn't *understand* where we were. *work out*
e You don't have to decide now. *Consider* it carefully and let me know tomorrow. *think over*
f Not a word they said was true – they *invented* the whole story. *made up*

See also the Phrasal verbs reference section on the last page of the book.

WRITING SKILLS: Reference: *this* and *which*

1 **Look at these examples. Notice how** *it* **and** *they* **refer back to single nouns, but** *this* **refers to complete ideas.**

   a I got a part-time job in a hotel. *It* wasn't very interesting, but I only had to work four days a week. *This* gave me plenty of time to travel and see the country.

   It = the job
   This = the fact that I only worked four days a week

   b Many people use nicotine chewing gum to help them give up smoking. As you chew the gum, *it* releases nicotine into your body through your mouth. *This* reduces your need to smoke a cigarette.

   it = the chewing gum
   This = the process (of nicotine entering your body)

   c In 1917, the Bolsheviks seized power in Russia, and *they* immediately created a socialist dictatorship. *This* changed the course of Russian history for the next 70 years.

   they = the Bolsheviks
   This = what they did

   Instead of *This*, **we can use** *which* **to join these ideas.**

   a I only had to work four days a week, *which* gave me plenty of time to travel.
   b The chewing gum releases nicotine into your body, *which* reduces your need to smoke a cigarette.
   c In 1917, the Bolsheviks seized power, *which* changed the course of Russian history.

2 **Fill the gaps in these sentences with** *it*, *this* **or** *which*.

   a To save time, he decided to drive the wrong way up a one-way street, ... was a very dangerous thing to do.

   b He lost his temper and threw a bottle at me. Fortunately, ... just missed me.

   c In West Africa, people may avoid looking you in the eye. .... is not rude, but a sign of respect.

   d It snowed during the night, ... made it more difficult to find survivors of the plane crash.

3 **Match these pairs of ideas, and join them using** *This* **or** *which*.

   Many new cars have power steering …   … completely changed my life.
   Parking is limited to two hours in the city centre …   … is a very romantic way to see the town.
   In 1812, Napoleon decided to invade Russia …   … makes them much easier to park.
   In Luxor you can hire a horse-drawn carriage …   … makes it almost impossible for them to sink.
   At the age of 18 I won £100,000 …   … turned out to be a serious mistake.
   Most yachts have compartments filled with air … … encourages people to go to work by bus.

   a ....
   b ....
   c ....
   d ....
   e ....
   f ....

Unit 10 Describing things

11 The future

A Optimism and pessimism

What predictions do you think (a) an optimist and (b) a pessimist would make in these situations? Make predictions with *will* or *won't*. Use active and passive forms.

Future active & passive		
They'll (probably) / They (probably) won't		sell the car.
The car	will (probably) / (probably) won't	be sold.

Example: You're stuck in a lift.
Optimist: We'll be rescued soon.
Pessimist: We'll probably be here till morning.

1 You're having a barbecue on Saturday night.
   Optimist: The weather will be nice
   Pessimist: It's going to rain

2 Your plane is due to leave at exactly 10 o'clock tonight.
   Optimist: We leave at 10ʰ (on time) [sollte]
   Pessimist: It'll be delayed [probably]

3 You're wearing a parachute, and you're about to jump out of a plane.
   Optimist: I'll have a beautiful view
   Pessimist: my parachute won't open [probably]

4 You're about to go through customs, and you've got some diamonds hidden in your socks.
   Optimist: I think they won't to be found [Zoll]
   Pessimist: I think they'll find them

B Expect and hope

Look at your answers for each situation in Exercise A. Rewrite one using *I hope*, and the other using *I expect*.

Expect & hope	
I expect / I don't expect	they'll sell the car.
I hope	they('ll) sell the car. / they don't/won't sell the car.

Example: *I hope we'll be rescued soon. I expect we'll be here till morning.*

1 I hope we can have a barbecue on Saturday night
   I hope we don't have to cancel the barbecue because of the weather

2 I expect the plane leaves exactly at 10 o'clock tonight
   I don't expect the plane cannot leave at the right time

3 I hope I'll have a beautiful view
   I hope I don't be afraid to jump out of the plane

4 I hope the diamonds won't be found
   I hope I can past the customs without controll my socks

C Will be doing and will have done

Look at these newspaper cuttings from the future, and say what *will have happened* and what people *will be doing* by the end of the 21st century. If you like, add some ideas of your own.

> **Will be doing & will have done**
>
> This time next week, I'll **be sitting** on a beach.
> By the time I'm 50, my children **will have left** home.
> I'll **be doing** exams all next week, but by the time you arrive I **will have finished** them.

THE COLD WAR ENDS
Scientists have found a cure for the common cold. At the
January, 2076

IT'S PEACE AT LAST
The Third World War is over. At a peace treaty signed last
May, 2092

JAPANESE ASTRONAUTS LAND ON MARS
March, 2087

SHARES IN PLASTICS RISE
Yesterday's announcement that 70% of buildings are now made of plastic sent plastics shares sharply upwards
February, 2083

WORLD POPULATION REACHES 20 BILLION
June, 2080

OIL WILL RUN OUT IN TEN YEARS' TIME
August, 2069

NEW MOON CITY OPENED
The 100th city on the Moon was declared open yesterday. President Rousseau, who flew to the Moon for the opening ceremony, told the 250,000 new settlers that this was a
December, 2099

GOODBYE PETROL – HELLO ELECTRICITY
From midnight, petrol-driven cars will become illegal in cities. Only electric cars will now be permitted in
March, 2077

WHAT A LAZY LIFE!
People are only working an average of 20 weeks a year, according to a survey published today. The average family takes 7 holidays a year, with the Atlantic and Pacific undersea holiday cities being by far the most popular holiday destinations.
February, 2086

By the end of the 21st century, most people will be living in plastic houses.
The Third World War will have finished. Oil will have
....
....
....
....
....
....
....
....

D Giving reasons

Complete these sentences.

Example: You should speak slowly and clearly, in case ...
... their English isn't very good.

> You should take some sandwiches ...
> ... because the restaurant might be closed.
> ... in case the restaurant's closed.
> ... so that you don't get hungry.
> ... Otherwise, you might get hungry.

1 I'd better go to bed now. Otherwise ....
2 Write your name and address on your luggage, in case ....
3 You should take a warm sleeping bag, because ....
4 You'd better phone before you go. Otherwise ....
5 I'll give you an alarm clock, so that ....
6 We'd better buy some candles, in case ....
7 Make sure you've got some cash with you, because ....
8 Write the address on a piece of paper, so that ....

TRANSLATION

Translate into your own language:

1 By the time we get there, everyone will have gone home.

2 – How will I recognise you?
   – I'll be standing at the information desk and I'll be wearing a green hat.

3 You'd better take some cash in case they don't accept credit cards.

Now cover up the left-hand side, and translate your sentences back into English.

LISTENING: When I'm 60 …

You will hear someone imagining his life at the age of 60.

1 Listen and decide which of these statements are true and which are false (Write *T* or *F*).

   a He's not very keen on sport.
   b He's good at gardening.
   c He's already married and has a large family.
   d He doesn't like children very much.
   e He wants to travel before he settles down.
   f He expects to have a long and healthy life.

2 Here is a description of the picture he has of himself. Listen again and complete the missing words.

He's sitting on a .... looking out on a huge .... that he has .... himself. He has .... with someone he likes, and there are .... all around. Although he's 60, he's still very .... and goes .... whenever he can.

PRONUNCIATION: Stress in sentences

1 Listen to these two-line conversations. Notice where the stress comes.

   – Where shall we meet?   – When are they coming?
   – At the station.   – In an hour.

   – Where are you going?   – What are you eating?
   – To town to buy a dress. – Chicken and rice.

2 Look at these conversations. Which words will be stressed? Underline them.

   a – Where's my bag?
      – On the table.
   b – What's the time?
      – Five past six.
   c – What are you doing on Saturday?
      – I'm going to a party.
   d – Are you ready?
      – I'll come in a minute.
   e – Where's the butter?
      – It's in the fridge.
   f – What nationality is he?
      – I think he's Greek.
   g – What does he look like?
      – He's got a beard.

   Now listen and practise saying the conversations.

READING: Crossing the Sahara

Here is some advice to people who want to cross the Sahara Desert. Read the texts and answer the questions.

Scorpions are common in the Sahara. They like cool, dark places, such as the inside of an empty shoe. They are also active at night: if you have a comfortable roof-rack with a wooden floor, this might be a good place to sleep.

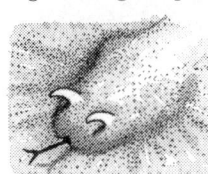

And watch out for the horned viper. This is a very poisonous snake which lies just below the surface of the sand with his horns sticking up, waiting for insects and small animals to come by. He doesn't enjoy being trodden on.

Driving in sand needs special techniques. Tyre pressures should be lowered considerably. It is quite an experience to be in an ordinary VW bus, stopped before a vast sea of deep soft sand, and know for certain that it will never get across; then to lower tyre pressures far below the normal minimum – and just cruise across to the other side with no problem at all. Don't forget to pump the tyres up once you are on safe, hard ground again.

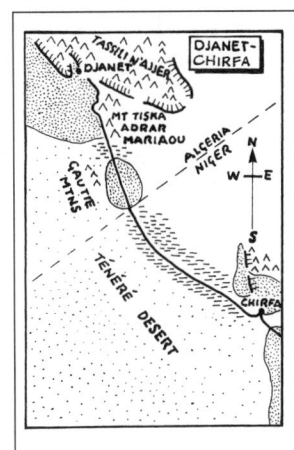

One of the most dangerous routes is the 550 km from Djanet to Chirfa. It is dangerous not so much because of what it will do to you or your vehicle but because it is so lonely, especially in summer. In fact, it is almost impossible to get lost because the route is very well marked. However, if your vehicle breaks down half way along the route, it might be three months before another vehicle passes, and it is impossible to walk to safety. Therefore you must get that vehicle going again, or die.

In many places, lots of little children will surround you and ask for 'presents'. If a little boy has been helpful in giving directions, for instance, then by all means give him some sweets or a ball-point pen. But if you just stop and hand out gifts, this could cause a commotion – even a riot. And it will spoil things for other tourists who may not have lots of cheap gifts to hand out.

Never carry petrol in plastic jerry-cans. Firstly, petrol can react with the plastic and make it unsafe. Secondly, when petrol gets very hot and shaken up, it changes to gas, and tremendous pressures can build up. Plastic jerrycans are not strong enough to contain this pressure: they swell up and crack, allowing gas to escape, and could easily cause an explosion.

If you arrive at a Tuareg village, take your time about introductions and greetings. They have all the time in the world. Soon very small glasses will be laid out, and a pot of tea will be put on a small fire. Do not go away. Stay, and you will be offered these small glasses of very sweet tea. Still do not go away. Each glass of tea must be drunk fairly quickly, and with much enjoyment. If after the third round of tea, no more is offered, this means that you are welcome, and welcome to stay for a while. If a fourth round of tea is offered, it means that you are welcome but not asked to stay, as it is not convenient. Drink this fourth glass, and slowly, politely say goodbye and go.

Adapted from the *Sahara Handbook* by Simon Glen, published by Lascelles.

1 Why should you
   a wear shoes when walking in sand?
   b shake shoes before putting them on?

2 What is dangerous about the Djanet-Chirfa route?
   – it's easy to get lost
   – it will damage your vehicle
   – if you break down, you can't walk to safety

3 In a Tuareg village, what should you do if
   a they start making tea?
   b you are offered a fourth cup of tea?

4 Which of the following are good pieces of advice?
   a Don't attempt to cross areas of deep sand.
   b Keep petrol in metal jerrycans.
   c When you meet small children, give them presents.
   d Sleep on your roof-rack.
   e It is essential that you know how to repair your own vehicle.

Unit 11 The future 55

12 Accidents

A Bad luck

The pictures show what some people were doing just before they had accidents. Say what they were doing and what happened. Use the expressions in the box to help you.

break
burn
choke
cut
fall over
get an electric shock
get stuck
set on fire
slip
twist

1 *She was walking down the street when she slipped on a banana skin. She* ....

2 ....

3 ....

4 ....

5 ....

6 ....

B Dos and don'ts

Write two things that you *should* do and one that you *shouldn't* do in these situations.

1 Someone has a heart attack.

   Call an ambulance.
   ....
   ....

2 You see smoke coming in under the front door of your third floor flat.

   ....
   ....
   ....

3 You get bitten on the leg by a snake.

   ....
   ....
   ....

C On the road

Write the answers in the diagram. All the answers go across except for number 10, which goes down.

1 If you try to stop quickly on a wet or icy road, you may do this. (4) *schleudern*

2 Some people don't do this before they turn left or right. (8) *blinken*

3 Another word for a car *accident*. (5)

4 The accident was your *Schuld*, not mine! (5)

5 You might have to do this to avoid a child who runs out in front of your car. (6) *ausweichen*

6 Put your foot on pedal B if you want to do this. (5) *bremsen*

7 Pedestrians can be *überfahren* .... by careless drivers. (3, 4)

8 Put your foot on pedal A if you want to do this. (10) *beschleunigen*

9 Make sure there's nothing coming the other way before you .... another car. (8) *überholen*

10 If you're on the road, make sure you've got plenty of .... (9) *Versicherung*

Crossword answers:
1. SKID
2. INDICATE
3. CRASH
4. FAULT
5. SWERVE
6. BRAKE
7. RUN OVER
8. ACCELERATE
9. OVERTAKE
10. (down) INSURANCE

New words

Use this space to write down new words from the unit, with your own notes and examples.

Unit 12 Accidents

TRANSLATION

Translate into your own language:

1 Quick! The house is on fire! Call the fire brigade!

2 – What have you done to your foot?
– I twisted my ankle while I was running for a bus.

3 He skidded on the ice and crashed into a parked car.

Now cover up the left-hand side, and translate your sentences back into English.

LISTENING: Narrow escapes
Knappes Entkommen

1 🎧 You will hear the opening sentences of two 'narrow escape' stories. Listen to the recording.

Now look at the questions below. Try to guess what the answers are.

Story A
a What was the boy doing?
b What did she do?
c Where did the axe hit her?
d What did she do?
e What did the doctor do?

Story B
a What happened one night?
b Why couldn't they get out of the front door?
c Why couldn't they call for help?
d How did they feel?
e What did the mountain rescue team do?
f Why were they surprised?

2 🎧 Listen to the two stories and answer the questions.

PHRASAL VERBS: Transitive verbs (3)

1 Look at these sentences. Match them with the openings in the box.
a 5.. he *let* me *down*. *im Stich lassen*
b 2.. he *knocked* me *out*.
c 1.. he keeps *putting* me *down*.
d 4. I can't *make* him *out*. *einschätzen*
e 6. he *talked* me *round*.
f 3. he nearly *ran* me *over*.

c	1	I hate talking to him because …
b	2	He hit me over the head and …
f	3	I was crossing the road when …
d	4	He's very mysterious –
a	5	I trusted him but …
e	6	I didn't want to go with him but …

2 The phrasal verbs in these sentences are mixed up. Change them so that they make better sense.

a Mind that dog! You nearly *knocked* it *out*!
b A brick fell on his head and *put* him *down*.
c I can't *let* her *down* at all. She's very strange.
d Don't *talk* me *round*. I'm just as clever as you.
e He doesn't want to sell it, but I'll try and *make* him *out*.
f I'll expect you at 12. Don't *run* me *over*, will you?

See also the Phrasal verbs reference section on the last page of the book.

Unit 12 Accidents

WRITING SKILLS: Joining ideas: clauses and phrases

1 Look at these examples.

A My leg was injured, *so* I couldn't play in the match.
  I couldn't play in the match *because* my leg was injured.
  I couldn't play in the match *because of* my injured leg.

B His leg was injured, *but* he carried on walking.
  He carried on walking *although* his leg was injured.
  He carried on walking *in spite of* his injured leg.

C Her leg was injured. *Otherwise* she was physically fit.
  She was physically fit, *except that* her leg was injured.
  She was physically fit, *except for* / *apart from* her injured leg.

2 Fill the gaps so that the sentences in the two columns mean the same.

a Although ...., he wasn't chosen to be ambassador to Taiwan.
  In spite of his knowledge of Chinese, he wasn't chosen to be ambassador to Taiwan.

b She still has excellent hearing although she's very old.
  She still has excellent hearing in spite of *being old*.

c We decided not to go sailing because the weather was bad.
  We decided not to go sailing because of *bad weather*.

d He's very well qualified for the job, except that *he hasn't enough experience*.
  He's very well qualified for the job, except for his lack of experience.

e Tourists have been warned not to go there because there's a risk of catching malaria.
  Tourists have been warned not to go there because of *the risk of malaria*.

3 Join these ideas using words from the box. If necessary, change the order of the sentences, and make any other changes you like.

| and | because | although | except that | apart from |
| but | because of | in spite of | except for | Otherwise |

a The weather was bad.
  We decided to go camping.
  We had a wonderful time.

b It's very noisy.
  There are frequent traffic jams.
  I enjoy living in Cairo.

c She had good qualifications.
  She wasn't given the job.
  She was too old.

d It was Saturday evening.
  The café was completely empty.
  There was a couple at a corner table.

Unit 12 Accidents   59

Review: Units 7–12

1 Sentence rewriting

Rewrite these sentences using the words given.

Example:
They deliver 300 million letters every day.
300 million letters *are delivered every day.*

1 I used to live in Canada.
   .... any longer.
2 They've opened a new bypass.
   A new bypass ....
3 Someone repaired my TV last week.
   I had ....
4 It's a pity that we don't have a video camera.
   I wish ....
5 You correct typing mistakes with Tipp-Ex.
   Tipp-Ex is used ....
6 In my opinion, they won't arrive on time.
   .... expect ....
7 Leave early because the roads might be crowded.
   Leave early in case ....

2 Verb forms

Write the correct form of the verbs.

Example:
His wallet *was stolen* (steal) while he was standing in a queue at the post office.

1 – .... (*you* write) that letter yet?
  – Yes. I .... (post) it last night.
2 He .... (be) very thin, but now
  he .... (grow) quite fat.
3 If I .... (have) enough money, I'd buy a Picasso.
4 You .... (*not* like) it if someone spoke to you like that.
5 I wish I .... (can) swim.
6 If you come late again, you .... (punish).
7 By this time next week we .... (finish) all our exams, and we .... (lie) on the beach sunbathing!

3 Vocabulary

1 Where would you have
   a your car serviced? ....
   b your eyes tested? ....
   c your iron repaired? ....

2 Match the verbs with the nouns.

   dial   a library
   fill in   the receiver
   join   a parcel
   lift   a number
   wrap   a customs form

3 What would you use these things for?
   a a car jack ....
   b chopsticks ....
   c bathroom scales ....
   d a pair of pliers ....

4 Name the objects in the pictures.
   a ....
   b ....
   c ....
   d ....
   e ....

5 Match the items on the left with those on the right.

   accelerate   to avoid hitting someone
   brake   to go faster
   overtake   on an icy road
   run over   to slow down
   skid   a pedestrian
   swerve   a slow-moving vehicle

4 Fill the gaps

Fill each gap with *one* suitable word. Example:

I ......*was*...... walking through the park yesterday when I suddenly ......*heard*...... a loud scream.

1 – What would you do ......*if*...... a snake ......*bit*...... you on the leg?
 – I'd try not to ......*move*...... around too much, ...*so*...... that the poison wouldn't spread too quickly. And if I ......*had*...... a knife, I'd cut the wound open and suck ......*out*...... the poison.

2 I'd like some of that yellow ......*stuff*...... – you know, it's ......*made*...... from vegetable oil, and you spread it ......*on*...... bread instead of butter. Um, *margarine* – that's what it's ......*called*......

3 By the end of the 21st century, scientists will probably ......*have*...... found a cure for cancer, and we'll probably all be ......*flying*...... off to the moon for our summer holidays. They ......*may*...... even have found a way to stop us killing each other in wars – I ......*hope*...... so, anyway.

4 A friend of mine had a ......*narrow*...... escape last week. He fell asleep ......*while*...... he was watching TV, and his cigarette ......*fell*...... on the carpet and ......*set*...... it on fire. Luckily, a neighbour saw ......*smoke*...... coming out of the window and called the fire ......*brigade*......

5 Writing paragraphs

Write a short paragraph (two or three sentences) on the following:

1 Think about the place where you live. How has it changed in the past few years?

2 A visitor to your country wants to know how to make a phone call home. Tell him/her what to do.

3 Think about what's in the news this week. What do you think will happen *next* week?

4 What should you do to help if someone has a heart attack?

6 Dictation

You will hear someone talking about the town where he lives, and how it has changed.

Listen and write down what you hear.

13 Comparing and evaluating

A Small and big differences

Write sentences that mean the same as the words in *italics*.

Example:
He's better-looking than I am, but *I'm much more intelligent*.
He isn't nearly as intelligent as I am.

Small differences		
Mary's	slightly / a bit	taller (than John).
John isn't quite as tall (as Mary).		

Big differences		
Mary's	much / far	more interesting (than John).
John isn't nearly as interesting (as Mary).		

1 Cars aren't as much fun as motorbikes, but *motorbikes are far more dangerous*.
   Cars aren't ...as dangerous as motorbikes...

2 CDs sound better than cassettes, but *cassettes aren't quite as expensive*.
   CDs are ...much more expensive than cassettes...

3 *Greek isn't nearly as useful as English*, but it's a very beautiful language.
   English is ...much more useful than Greek...

4 German mustard tastes very similar to French mustard, but *German mustard is slightly hotter*.
   French mustard isn't ...as hot as German mustard...

5 *The bus takes a bit longer than the train*, but it's a lot cheaper.
   The train doesn't ...take as long as the bus...

6 I don't see why he got the job instead of me. *My qualifications are far better than his*.
   His qualifications aren't ...as good as mine...

B Comparison of adjectives and adverbs

Which of these words are adjectives and which are adverbs? Which could be either? Write *Adj*, *Adv* or *AA*.

1	good	5	fast
2	well	6	clearly
3	friendly	7	comfortable
4	hard	8	funny

Adjectives ...
He's a **fluent** speaker. → He's a **more fluent** speaker than I am.
She's a **hard** worker. → She's a **harder** worker than I am.

... and adverbs
He speaks **fluently**. → He speaks **more fluently** than I do.
She works **hard**. → She works **harder** than I do.

Now fill the gaps in these sentences with comparative forms of the words in the box.

1 You're a ...better... cook than I am. Why don't you cook lunch?
2 You're playing ...more well... than you were a few months ago.
3 Our new neighbours are ...more friendly... than the old ones.
4 We'll all have to try a bit ...harder...
5 She can run ...more faster... than anyone else in the school.
6 I can see much ...more clearly... with these new glasses.
7 Why don't you sit in this chair. You'd be much ...more comfortable...
8 Don't you know any ...more funny... jokes than that?

C Too and enough

Tom had a bad time last week. Here are some of the things that happened to him. Write two sentences about each one, using *too* and *enough*. Use the words in brackets in your answers.

Too and enough

They've got **too** many children.
They haven't got **enough** bedrooms.

Their flat | is **too** small.
           | isn't big **enough**.

They're **too** poor | to move house.
They're not rich **enough** |

Example: He wanted a £7,000 car, but he only had £5,000.
The car was too expensive. (expensive)
He didn't have enough money (to buy it). (money)

1 He sat on a chair and it broke under his weight.
.... (heavy)
.... (strong)

2 He received a letter written in Spanish, and he could only understand a bit of it.
The letter was too .... (difficult)
His Spanish wasn't good enough .... (good)

3 He tried to climb a mountain, but half way up he had to give up.
.... (high)
.... (fit)

4 He did an exam with 20 questions, but he only had time to do 15 of them.
.... (questions)
.... (time)

D I'd rather ...

Look at the example, and write a similar answer to one of the questions below.

Example: Would you rather have a car or a motorbike?

Motorbikes cost less than cars, and they're cheaper to run. They're also faster. On the other hand, they're much more dangerous than cars, and they're not very pleasant to ride in bad weather. And you can carry more people in a car, and a lot more luggage. So on the whole I'd rather have a car.

Would you rather ...

... have a word-processor or a typewriter?
... live in Britain or the USA?
... have a TV or a radio?
... go camping or stay in a hotel?
... cook a meal or wash the dishes?
... be a student or a teacher?
... be male or female?

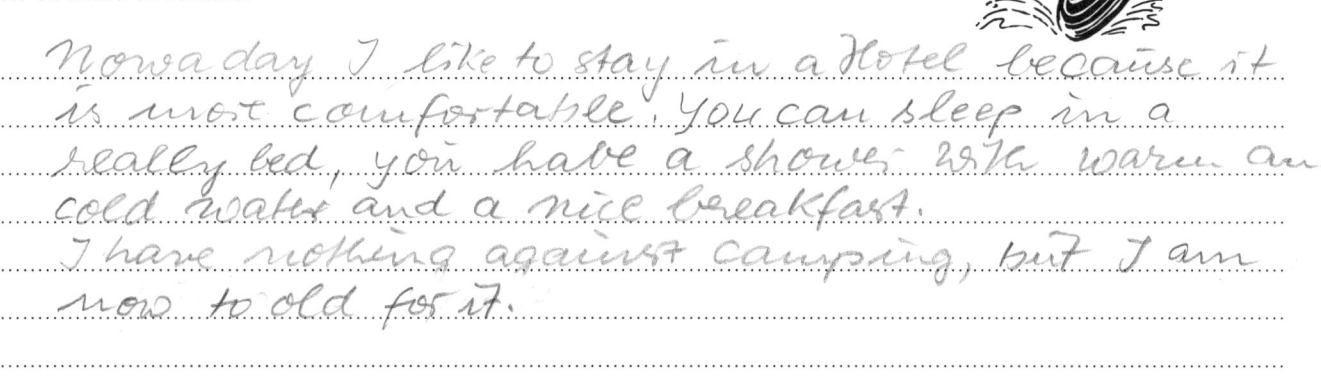

Nowaday I like to stay in a Hotel because it is most comfortable. You can sleep in a really bed, you have a shower with warm and cold water and a nice breakfast.
I have nothing against camping, but I am now to old for it.

Unit 13 Comparing and evaluating

TRANSLATION

Translate into your own language:

1 He works much harder than he used to.

....
....

2 Windsurfing's OK, but it isn't nearly as much fun as water-skiing.

....
....
....

3 Are you sure there's enough food for everyone?

....
....

Now cover up the left-hand side, and translate your sentences back into English.

LISTENING: Living in Britain

1 You will hear people from Poland, France and New Zealand saying what they find strange about living in Britain.

Here are some of the things they say. Before you listen, find pairs of expressions that you think go together (e.g. *separate taps – wash your hands*).

separate taps	people stared
cross the street	change gears
bump into someone	wash your hands
left-hand-side driving	seeing the car coming
walking in my shorts	'Oh I'm really sorry'

Now listen and check your answers.

2 Listen again and answer the questions.

Speaker 1
a Why does she find separate taps a problem?
b Why can't she change gears?
c How does she feel when she crosses the street?

Speaker 2
a What are English people like?
b How do they behave in queues?

Speaker 3
a What was he wearing?
b What wasn't he wearing?
c Why did people stare?

PRONUNCIATION: Linking words: consonant + consonant

verbindend

1 Listen to these pairs of words. The first ends in a consonant sound, and the second begins with a consonant sound. Notice how they are linked together.

big girl	sit down	Government troops
red dog	take back	electric drill
phone bill	good boy	food processor
credit card	fast train	village square
desk top	art gallery	carving knife

2 Find links between words ending and beginning in a consonant sound in these sentences. Draw lines to connect them.

a Is it good luck to see a black cat?
b The next train to Prague goes in ten minutes.
c The clock said ten past two.
d I bought two bedside tables and some red curtains.
e We had fish soup and French bread.
f Like most people, I sometimes feel lonely.

Now listen and practise saying the sentences.

READING: Left-handedness

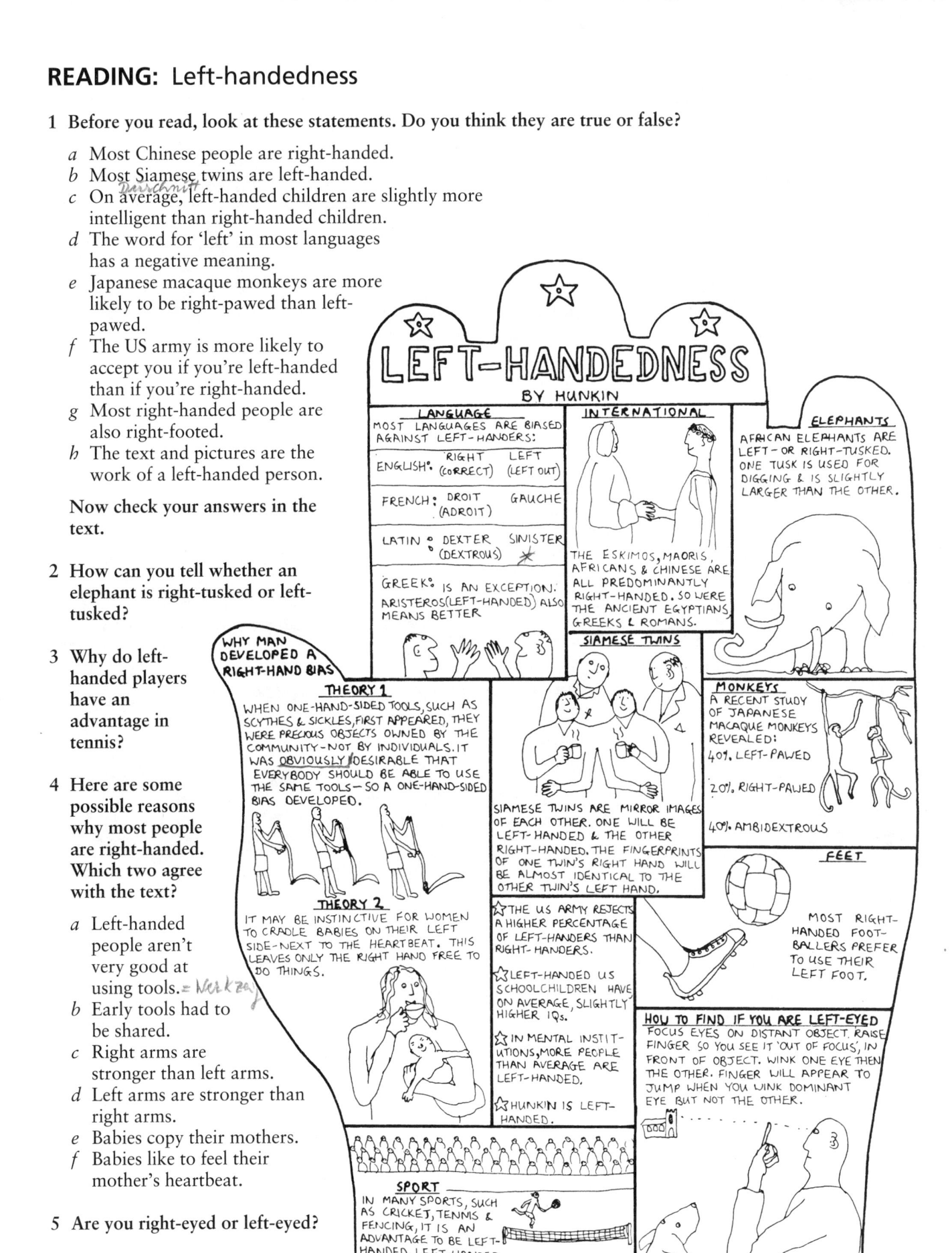

1 Before you read, look at these statements. Do you think they are true or false?

   a Most Chinese people are right-handed.
   b Most Siamese twins are left-handed.
   c On average, left-handed children are slightly more intelligent than right-handed children.
   d The word for 'left' in most languages has a negative meaning.
   e Japanese macaque monkeys are more likely to be right-pawed than left-pawed.
   f The US army is more likely to accept you if you're left-handed than if you're right-handed.
   g Most right-handed people are also right-footed.
   h The text and pictures are the work of a left-handed person.

   Now check your answers in the text.

2 How can you tell whether an elephant is right-tusked or left-tusked?

3 Why do left-handed players have an advantage in tennis?

4 Here are some possible reasons why most people are right-handed. Which two agree with the text?

   a Left-handed people aren't very good at using tools.
   b Early tools had to be shared.
   c Right arms are stronger than left arms.
   d Left arms are stronger than right arms.
   e Babies copy their mothers.
   f Babies like to feel their mother's heartbeat.

5 Are you right-eyed or left-eyed?

LEFT-HANDEDNESS
BY HUNKIN

LANGUAGE
MOST LANGUAGES ARE BIASED AGAINST LEFT-HANDERS:

ENGLISH: RIGHT (CORRECT) LEFT (LEFT OUT)

FRENCH: DROIT (ADROIT) GAUCHE

LATIN: DEXTER (DEXTROUS) SINISTER

GREEK: IS AN EXCEPTION. ARISTEROS (LEFT-HANDED) ALSO MEANS BETTER

INTERNATIONAL
THE ESKIMOS, MAORIS, AFRICANS & CHINESE ARE ALL PREDOMINANTLY RIGHT-HANDED. SO WERE THE ANCIENT EGYPTIANS, GREEKS & ROMANS.

ELEPHANTS
AFRICAN ELEPHANTS ARE LEFT- OR RIGHT-TUSKED. ONE TUSK IS USED FOR DIGGING & IS SLIGHTLY LARGER THAN THE OTHER.

WHY MAN DEVELOPED A RIGHT-HAND BIAS

THEORY 1
WHEN ONE-HAND-SIDED TOOLS, SUCH AS SCYTHES & SICKLES, FIRST APPEARED, THEY WERE PRECIOUS OBJECTS OWNED BY THE COMMUNITY - NOT BY INDIVIDUALS. IT WAS OBVIOUSLY DESIRABLE THAT EVERYBODY SHOULD BE ABLE TO USE THE SAME TOOLS - SO A ONE-HAND-SIDED BIAS DEVELOPED.

THEORY 2
IT MAY BE INSTINCTIVE FOR WOMEN TO CRADLE BABIES ON THEIR LEFT SIDE - NEXT TO THE HEARTBEAT. THIS LEAVES ONLY THE RIGHT HAND FREE TO DO THINGS.

SIAMESE TWINS
SIAMESE TWINS ARE MIRROR IMAGES OF EACH OTHER. ONE WILL BE LEFT-HANDED & THE OTHER RIGHT-HANDED. THE FINGERPRINTS OF ONE TWIN'S RIGHT HAND WILL BE ALMOST IDENTICAL TO THE OTHER TWIN'S LEFT HAND.

☆ THE US ARMY REJECTS A HIGHER PERCENTAGE OF LEFT-HANDERS THAN RIGHT-HANDERS.

☆ LEFT-HANDED US SCHOOLCHILDREN HAVE ON AVERAGE, SLIGHTLY HIGHER IQs.

☆ IN MENTAL INSTITUTIONS, MORE PEOPLE THAN AVERAGE ARE LEFT-HANDED.

☆ HUNKIN IS LEFT-HANDED.

MONKEYS
A RECENT STUDY OF JAPANESE MACAQUE MONKEYS REVEALED:
40% LEFT-PAWED
20% RIGHT-PAWED
40% AMBIDEXTROUS

FEET
MOST RIGHT-HANDED FOOTBALLERS PREFER TO USE THEIR LEFT FOOT.

HOW TO FIND IF YOU ARE LEFT-EYED
FOCUS EYES ON DISTANT OBJECT. RAISE FINGER SO YOU SEE IT 'OUT OF FOCUS' IN FRONT OF OBJECT. WINK ONE EYE THEN THE OTHER. FINGER WILL APPEAR TO JUMP WHEN YOU WINK DOMINANT EYE BUT NOT THE OTHER.

SPORT
IN MANY SPORTS, SUCH AS CRICKET, TENNIS & FENCING, IT IS AN ADVANTAGE TO BE LEFT-HANDED. LEFT-HANDED PLAYERS GET USED TO RIGHT-HANDED OPPONENTS, BUT RIGHT-HANDED PLAYERS ARE OFTEN CONFUSED BY A LEFT-HANDED OPPONENT.

MOST RIGHT-HANDERS ARE RIGHT-EYED. THERE IS SOME EVIDENCE THAT THEY ALSO CHEW MORE WITH THE RIGHT SIDE OF THE JAW.

From *Almost Everything There is to Know*, by Hunkin, published by Hamlyn.

14 The media

A Which page?

On which page(s) would you expect to find these newspaper extracts? Write the page numbers in the spaces provided.

ON OTHER PAGES

Home news	2–5
International news	6–10
Financial news	11–12
Leading articles	13
Letters	14
Arts & Entertainment	15–16
Obituaries	17
Classified advertisements	17
Horoscope	18
Cartoons	18
TV and Radio	19–20
Sport	21–24
Weather	24
Crossword	24

1 page ...17....
After leaving university she joined a law firm, but her real love was politics, and at the age of 29 she became Labour Member of Parliament for

2 page ....
13 Farm animal (5)

3 page ....
Sir,
I am writing to complain about

4 page ....
A 10-year-old girl was in hospital last night after she

5 page ....
Capricorn
Although you could be having problems at work this week, your social life has never been better.

6 page ....
CHAMPIONS LOSE 2-1

7 page ....
Tonight temperatures will drop to around 3° in the north, but in the south they will stay around 8°. Rain

8 page ....
The US dollar dropped nearly 2 pfennigs against the German mark

9 page ....
8.00 That's Showbiz! *Boring chat show presented by Leonora*

10 page ....
American officials flew to Moscow yesterday for urgent discussions

11 page ....
FOR SALE 1992 Ford Escort 4-door

12 page ....
It is always a pleasure to hear Emily Baker sing in a title role, and last night's performance in *Carmen* was

13 page ....
This time the Government has gone too far. When will they realise that they were elected to serve the people

14 page ....

B TV programmes

Write about two programmes that you watch (or don't watch!) on TV. Say what kind of programme it is and what you like and don't like about it.

cartoon	crime series	news
chat show	documentary	soap
comedy	game show	sports

Example: *'That's Showbiz!' is a popular chat show. It has two or three film stars each week, and a singer or group. It's usually very boring, but sometimes one of the guests is quite interesting, and they often have good music.*

1 ....

2 ....

C Understanding the headlines

Read the information about newspaper headlines in the box. Then look at the headlines below and explain what they mean.

Headlines: a rough guide
The Present simple = someone **has done** something **UNEMPLOYED MAN WINS £1M** *means* An unemployed man has won a million pounds
The Past participle = something **has been done** **THREE KILLED IN HOUSE FIRE** *means* Three people have been killed in a house fire
The infinitive = something **is going to happen** **PM TO VISIT CHINA** *means* The Prime Minister is going to visit China

1. **MONA LISA STOLEN**
2. **NEW SHAKESPEARE PLAY DISCOVERED**
3. **BANK MANAGER DISAPPEARS WITH £1M**
4. **12-YEAR-OLD CLIMBS EVEREST**
5. **ELECTRICITY PRICES TO RISE BY 150%**
6. **WHITE HOUSE DAMAGED BY BOMB**
7. **BRITAIN TO BECOME REPUBLIC ON JAN 1**
8. **CHIMPANZEE WINS CHESS GAME**

1 ....
2 ....
3 ....
4 ....
5 ....
6 ....
7 ....
8 ....

New words

Use this space to write down new words from the unit, with your own notes and examples.

Unit 14 The media

TRANSLATION

Translate into your own language:

1 I put an advertisement in the local paper, but no-one answered it.

2 – Is *Women Today* a monthly magazine?
– No, it comes out once a fortnight.

3 – Is there anything good on TV tonight?
– Yes. There's a documentary on after the news.

Now cover up the left-hand side, and translate your sentences back into English.

LISTENING: Media habits

1 🔲 You will hear two people talking about how they use the media. What do they read, watch and listen to? Listen and complete the tables.

Speaker 1	
Newspaper	
Magazines	
TV	
Radio	

Speaker 2	
Newspaper	
Magazines	
TV	
Radio	

2 Which speaker might say these things? (Write *1*, *2* or *Both*.)

a 'I like to follow the news.'
b 'I think television is rather a waste of time.'
c 'I do the crossword every day.'
d 'I love listening to the radio.'
e 'I like to relax and watch a good thriller.'
f 'I find science very interesting.'
g 'I'm a lecturer in Business Studies in Edinburgh.'

PHRASAL VERBS: Double meanings

1 Each of the phrasal verbs can have two of the meanings given below. Match them, using a dictionary to help you.

give away ....   look up ....
turn down ....   pick up ....
bring up ....   put up ....

a have (s.o.) to stay   g collect, meet
b reveal a secret   h make quieter
c introduce a topic   i visit (after a long time)
d take from the floor   j build, construct
e give to other people   k try to find (in a book)
f raise (a child)   l say 'no' to someone

2 🔲 Listen to the recording. Which meaning of the phrasal verb do you hear each time?

3 Complete these sentences using a phrasal verb.

a He applied for promotion, but they ...
b I don't know the French for 'tape recorder'. Why don't we ...
c I don't need all these old clothes. I think I'll ...
d We've got a spare room. We can ...
e The radio's keeping me awake. Could you ...
f He lives in Mexico City. If you're going there, why don't you ...
g Just leave your suitcases at the school. I'm going that way, so I can ...
h My parents died when I was a baby, so my grandparents ...

See also the Phrasal verbs reference section on the last page of the book.

WRITING SKILLS: Similarities

1 Look at these examples.

Tanya comes from a large family, *and so* does her husband.
Both Tanya and her husband | come from large families.
Tanya and her husband *both* |

New York is a violent city, *and so* are Washington and Miami.
New York, Washington and Miami are *all* violent cities.

Compared with most countries, Norway *doesn't* have serious economic problems, *and nor* does Sweden.
Compared with most countries, *neither* Norway *nor* Sweden has serious economic problems.

2 Make sentences like those in the examples about

   a   tobacco and alcohol

   ....

   b   lions and wolves

   ....

   c   Tokyo, Hong Kong and Singapore

   ....

   d   Abraham Lincoln and John F Kennedy

   ....

3 Notice how we can develop the sentences in Part 1 into paragraphs.

Tanya and her husband both come from large families. *Both of them* have living grandparents and a large number of uncles, aunts and cousins.

New York, Washington and Miami are all violent cities. *In all three cities* there's a high crime rate and it's dangerous to walk in the streets at night.

Compared with most countries, neither Norway nor Sweden has serious economic problems. *Both countries* have small populations and plenty of natural resources.

4 Write similar paragraphs based on these notes.

   a   John/Richard – talented musicians. Good singing voices. Play several different instruments.

   b   Mars/Jupiter – not able to support life. Very cold. No oxygen in atmosphere.

   c   Christianity/Islam/Buddhism – major world religions. Have spread through many countries. Millions of followers. Influence on art and literature.

15 Recent events

A Personal news

Write paragraphs based on the notes in the boxes.

Example:

I've won £5,000 in the national lottery. The money arrived yesterday. I haven't decided how to spend it yet, but I'll probably buy a motorbike and go on a long holiday.

win £5,000 in national lottery
money arrive yesterday
not decide how to spend it
probably buy motorbike – go on long holiday

1 ....

finally arrive in Turkey
get here yesterday
not very good trip – break down twice
find lovely little apartment by the sea
food good – sea warm
everyone very friendly

2 ....

give up smoking
two weeks ago
very difficult at first
now much easier
put on a lot of weight
never smoke again

Now write about a real piece of news about yourself.

3 ....

B Asking questions

Look at these news items, and ask questions based on the notes in the boxes. For each item, add a question of your own.

1 Thieves have broken into a bank and stolen £2,000,000.

Who did it?
How did they get in? They got...
Have they been caught?

> Someone did it. They got in somehow. Either they've been caught or they haven't.

2 A light plane has crashed.

What caused the crash?
Were there any people killed on board?
Where did it happen?

> Something caused the crash. It happened somewhere. Either the people on board were killed or they weren't.

3 A manned spacecraft has landed on Mars.

When did they arrived?
How long did it take to get there?
Have they send back any photos?

> They arrived some time. It probably took a long time to get there. Maybe they've sent back some photos.

C What have they been doing?

Write sentences saying what these people *have been doing*.

Example: He's seen the news, a soap, and a movie.
He's been watching television.

> **Present perfect continuous**
> have/has been + -ing
> I've been **sitting** in the park.
> She's been **reading** a novel.

1 She's written to her grandmother, an old schoolfriend and her boyfriend.

2 They've polished the furniture, vacuumed the living room carpet and done the washing up.

3 He's done two workbook exercises, learned 10 irregular verbs and written a composition.

4 They've painted the bedroom ceiling and wallpapered the living room.

5 She's had a bath, changed her clothes and put on some make-up.

6 He's won one game of chess, drawn one game, and lost two games.

7 She's read the front page, the obituaries, and the sports news.

TRANSLATION

Translate into your own language:

1 They've won the election. I heard it on the news this afternoon.

2 – You look worn out.
  – I am a bit tired. I haven't been sleeping very well recently.

3 What's the matter with her? She's been behaving strangely all week.

....
....
....
....
....
....
....
....

Now cover up the left-hand side, and translate your sentences back into English.

LISTENING: What has happened?

1 Here are some key words from three telephone conversations. Which conversation do you think will be about
   – a car breaking down?
   – a party?
   – a driving test?

   a earrings – dolphin – dance – lounge – ring back
   b relief – examiner – relaxed – reversing – celebration
   c oil – battery – airport – borrow – insurance – favour

2 Now listen to the conversations and answer the questions.

Conversation 1
– What has happened?
– How did the woman spend the evening?
– What is the man going to do?

Conversation 2
– How does the man feel? Why?
– Why does the woman say 'third time lucky'?
– What are they going to do?

Conversation 3
– What has happened?
– What does the woman want to do? Why?
– Is it the first time this has happened? How do we know?

PRONUNCIATION: Changing stress

1 Listen to these two-line conversations. Notice how the stress changes in the replies.

– When shall we go?
– How about <u>next</u> week?

– I can't go this week.
– How about <u>next</u> week?

– Where's the suitcase?
– It's under the <u>bed</u>.

– Is it on the bed?
– It's <u>under</u> the bed.

2 Look at these conversations. Which words will be stressed in the replies? Underline them.

a – Let's get them a present.
  – I've bought some chocolates.

b – Shall we get some chocolates?
  – I've bought some chocolates.

c – I haven't seen you recently.
  – I've been on holiday.

d – When are you going on holiday?
  – I've been on holiday.

e – I'm thirsty.
  – Do you want some orange juice?

f – I don't like pineapple juice.
  – Do you want some orange juice?

Now listen and practise saying the conversations.

Unit 15 Recent events

READING: Personal letters

Here are parts of three letters to friends. The writers are Alan, Katrina and Jim.

Alan

I didn't realise there would be so much paperwork. First, you have to register with the police, and then there's the endless business of getting a resident's permit. I think I've spent half my time in the past month standing in queues! It must be terribly difficult for people who don't speak the language – it's really complicated and all of the forms are in German. Mine was pretty rusty when I arrived, but it's all coming back now.

Working hasn't been a problem. The 'office' is a spare bedroom containing one (old) word-processor and one (new) fax machine, which is all I need to keep in touch with the publishers back home.

The main difference about living here is that because it's much warmer, you're outside a lot more. For example, I've bought an old bike (new ones get stolen!) for getting around the city – I'm hardly using the car at all. And there are freshwater lakes nearby where the water's warm enough to swim in (they're good for sailing, too – but we haven't got a boat yet). Best of all, you're just up the road from the Alps. We've been quite a few times at the weekends: you take the cable car to the top of the mountain (where there's always a place you can have coffee!) and then walk down.

Katrina

You wouldn't believe the amount of stuff I've accumulated over the years. I've thrown away all the administrative papers, but have kept all the books and teaching materials – you never know, I might need them again. So there are now four crates and ten large boxes sitting in the front room. So I've got a great excuse if anyone asks me to do any work: I can't get across the room to my desk! It is cluttering the place up a bit, but it looks as if two of the children may be moving out over the next few months, so when that happens I'll just put it all into one of their rooms.

The best thing is that now I've actually got enough <u>time</u> to do what I want to do. Like lying in bed in the mornings, instead of jumping up and getting dressed at 7 o'clock. And doing a full 15 minutes of exercise every morning instead of the usual 3. And going into town in the afternoon and just wandering around and going into bookshops, and buying books that I <u>like</u> (rather than books that I need). And of course there's the theatre: I've been to three operas and two plays in the last two weeks alone. And it's great to have time at last to get in touch with old friends. It's so easy to lose touch.

Jim

The motorbike's great for getting around London in heavy traffic (though the insurance is incredibly expensive). I had a bit of a problem at first carrying the horn on the back, because it was wider than the bike, and I kept taking the wing mirrors off cars. So now I've had the horn cut in two, so I can carry it around in two bits and then screw it back together again when I arrive. It sounds just as good as it did before – to me at any rate.

Not much luck so far with the flat-hunting. All the places I like seem to be ridiculously expensive. Once you get further out towards Heathrow, there are some great places going quite cheap, but when you visit them you realise why – you can just about see the people waving from the planes as they go past. So I'm still looking.

Otherwise, there's not much going on. We don't finish till late most evenings, so the social life's suffering a bit. And there'll be no time – or money – to go on holiday this year. But as someone once said, 'Holidays are for people who don't like work.'

1 Choose an occupation for each of the writers.

actor	musician	teacher
bookseller	publisher	translator
climber	secretary	writer

2 According to the letters, who has/have ...

 a ... recently moved?
 b ... recently retired?
 c ... been getting fit?
 d ... been looking for somewhere to live?
 e ... been working in the evenings?
 f ... been going out a lot in the evenings?

3 Mark these statements *T* (= true), *F* (= false) or *?* (= can't tell).

 a Alan is German.
 b Alan has rented an office to work in.
 c Alan enjoys being in the open air.
 d Katrina lives alone.
 e Katrina is fond of reading.
 f Katrina hasn't got enough space at home.
 g Jim bought his motorbike second-hand.
 h Jim wants to live near Heathrow Airport.
 i Jim enjoys his work.

16 Teaching and learning

A School subjects

Look at the remarks in bubbles. What school subjects are the speakers talking about? Write them in the diagram, and then complete the sentence in number 10.

1. I enjoy learning about how people used to live, but I can never remember all the dates.

2. We listen to a lot of symphonies, but we don't actually learn to play any instruments ourselves.

3. Arithmetic and geometry were OK, but now we're doing algebra it's a bit more difficult.

4. At the moment, we're doing *King Lear*, and *Anna Karenina*.

5. Most of the time, we just draw and paint.

6. Today we had a test on mountains and deserts.

7. We learn about animals and plants – all living things.

8. We all do French, but we can also choose Russian or Chinese.

9. Well the formula for water is H_2O, and that means two atoms of hydrogen and one of oxygen.

10 I have to study too many subjects. Just look at my .... !

B School report

Which school subjects are (or were) you good at, and not so good at? Why? Write about three subjects.

Ability			
I'm	no good not very good quite good very good	at	sports English taking exams learning dates

Examples:

I'm quite good at maths. I like working with numbers and I can work things out in my head without using a calculator.

I'm not very good at history. I can never remember dates, and I mix up all the names of the kings and queens and politicians and battles.

1 ....
....
....

2 ....
....
....

3 ....
....
....

C What's the system?

Write about the education system in your country, using the questions as a guide.

At what age do children start primary school?

When do they start secondary school?

What different types of secondary school are there?

What's the school leaving age?

What are the most important school exams?

Do most people get a job when they leave school or do they go on to university or college?

How long does it take to get a university degree?

In Germany they start when they 6 years old they start when they around 10 years old There is a differenz between natural sience, expert knowledge (Realgymn.) Music school, grammar school (humanistic.)
The school leaving age is 15 years; intermediate qualification ≈ 16 years and 19-20y. from highschool. The most important school exams will be the school-leaving certificate Most people get a job when they leave school. To get a university degree takes minimum 6-8 semester, mostly more, it belongs to the faculty.

New words

Use this space to write down new words from the unit, with your own notes and examples.

Unit 16 Teaching and learning

TRANSLATION

Translate into your own language:

1 – Do you know how to type?
  – Yes, but I'm not very good at it.

2 You can only get a place at the secretarial college if you pass the entrance examination.

3 I'm a university graduate. I've got a degree in maths and physics.

....

Now cover up the left-hand side, and translate your sentences back into English.

LISTENING: Three school subjects

You will hear four people remembering subjects they did at school. They talk about biology, history and general science.

1 Here are some of the words they use. Which words do you think go with each subject? (Write B, H or S.)

- [ ] Latin names
- [ ] dates
- [ ] famous people
- [ ] battles
- [ ] equipment
- [ ] plants
- [ ] experiment
- [ ] emperors

🔊 Now listen and check your answers.

2 🔊 Listen again. Which of these statements are closest to what the four people say?

a We spent all our time learning facts by heart.
b We didn't learn much about real life.
c We had to copy words from the blackboard.
d The teacher made the subject seem real and interesting.
e We did lots of practice.
f We didn't have a chance to find things out for ourselves.

PHRASAL VERBS: Prepositional verbs (1)

1 The phrasal verbs in this exercise all have the form *verb + preposition*. These prepositions always come *before* a noun or pronoun.

Example: *look after*
I'll *look after* the children.
I'll *look after* them. (not ~~I'll look them after~~.)

2 Here are some common phrasal verbs with prepositions. Match them with their meanings.

look after	resemble
look into	collect, pick up
call for	find (by chance)
run into	meet (by chance)
come across	care for
take after	investigate
take to	like, be attracted to

3 The phrasal verbs in these sentences are mixed up. Change them so that they make better sense.

a I didn't *look into* him – he wasn't very friendly.
b I *called for* an interesting old travel guide in a second-hand bookshop yesterday.
c He's got a dog, but he doesn't *run into* it very well.
d The police are *coming across* the burglaries.
e I *look after* my mother – we have the same eyes.
f I'll *take to* you at 6.30. Make sure you're ready!
g I *took after* an old friend of mine the other day.

See also the Phrasal verbs reference section on the last page of the book.

Unit 16 Teaching and learning

WRITING SKILLS: Letter writing

1 Look at these openings to letters. Which person is

   a selling something?
   b applying for a job?
   c enquiring about places to stay?
   d writing to an old friend?
   e replying to a friend's letter?

1 Dear Sue,
   Many thanks for your letter – how nice to hear from you.

2 Dear Mr Bailey,
   I saw your advertisement in the Nursing Times for staff nurses in Canada.

3 Dear Richard,
   You may be surprised to get a letter from me after such a long time.

4 Dear Sir/Madam,
   I'm writing to ask you for information about accommodation in Scotland.

5 Dear Ms Howard,
   Thank you for your letter of 15th May, enclosing a cheque for £25.

2 Which of these sentences do you think continues each letter?

   a I'm glad to hear that you're all well and that the children are fine.
   b Unfortunately the jumper you ordered costs £30 including postage.
   c I've been meaning to write for ages, but somehow I never quite got round to it.
   d I'm thinking of staying there this summer, probably on the West coast.
   e I would like to apply for the job, and enclose a curriculum vitae.

3 Now look at these endings. Which openings in Part 1 could they go with?

   A I hope you'll be able to give me the information I need.
      Yours faithfully,

   B Well, that's all for now.
      Hope to hear from you soon.
      Love,

   C I look forward to hearing from you.
      Yours sincerely,

4 Choose one of these advertisements and write a letter. Use the examples above to help you.

BANANA T-SHIRTS FOR SALE
£15 each incl. postage.
Write to: T-Shirt Design, PO Box 54, Bristol BR2 2GD, England.

Luxury campsites in Northern Spain
For details write to:
Camping International,
25 Lombard Street,
London NW1A 2BR

WORK ON A YACHT THIS SUMMER
For details contact:
Bob Paterson, Cruise Crews, Box 153,
Kingston, Jamaica.

Unit 16 Teaching and learning

17 Narration

A What had happened?

Add a sentence to each item saying what *had happened*.

Example:
When I went down into the street, I couldn't find my car …

Someone had stolen it.
It had been stolen.

> **Past perfect active and passive**
>
> *Active*: had + Past participle
> Someone **had robbed** them.
> My car **had broken** down.
>
> *Passive*: had been + Past participle
> They **had been robbed**.
> The lights **had been left** on.

1 At the station, I jumped out of the taxi and ran onto the platform. But I was too late …
   ....

2 There was a man lying on the floor. As I got nearer I saw a neat round hole in the middle of his forehead …
   ....

3 I pushed the door, but it wouldn't open …
   ....

4 When I woke up, I found myself in a prison cell …
   ....

5 As soon as I got home, I went to get the diary from under the loose floorboard. It wasn't there …
   ....

6 When I showed the waitress a photo of Da Silva, she recognised it at once …
   ....

7 I smiled as Da Silva picked up the gun, pointed it at me and pulled the trigger. Nothing happened …
   ....

B Past states and previous actions

Write in the missing sentences.

	What were things like?	*What had happened?*
1	The coffee pot was empty.	Someone had drunk all the coffee.
2	The window was broken.	Someone had broken the window.
3	Her leg was bruised.	....
4	....	He'd washed his hands.
5	The light was on.	....
6	....	Someone had tidied the room.
7	It wasn't raining any more.	....
8	....	They had fallen asleep.

C Reported speech

Choose the most suitable speech bubble for each item, and complete the sentence using reported speech.

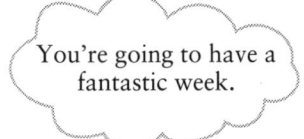

Actual words		Reported
does	→	did
is doing	→	was doing
can do	→	could do
will do	→	would do
did	→	had done
has done		

Speech bubbles:
- You're going to have a fantastic week.
- I won't put up taxes.
- I've only just had dinner.
- I haven't finished it yet.
- You'll have to have an operation.
- We're doing all we can to solve the case.
- I missed the last bus.
- I don't want to see you any more.

1 I offered him something to eat, but he said that *he had only just had dinner.*
2 In a TV interview, the President promised that ....
3 She got home at 2 a.m. and told her parents that ....
4 A police spokesman said that ....
5 She gave him back the ring and told him that ....
6 My horoscope was wrong, as usual. It said that ....
7 When I asked for my book back, he said that ....
8 I was horrified when the doctor told me that ....

D I realised …

Here are some scenes from stories in which people realised something. Write a short paragraph about each situation.

Example:

Jane was late. She arrived at the station just as the train was pulling out, and jumped on. Ten minutes later, the train stopped at a small station. Jane looked up from her book and read the name. Bottomley? Strange. They had never stopped there before. Then she realised that she was on the wrong train.

(Speech bubble: I'm on the wrong train!)

1 ....

(Speech bubble: Phew! It's only the cat!)

2 ....

(Speech bubble: I've left the tickets at home!)

Unit 17 Narration

TRANSLATION

Translate into your own language:

1 I suddenly realised that I hadn't locked the door. ....
....

2 I hardly recognised him when I saw him a year later – he had changed so much. ....
....
....

3 She promised she'd get in touch as soon as she arrived. ....
....

Now cover up the left-hand side, and translate your sentences back into English.

LISTENING: Locked in!

1 ▭ You will hear someone talking about how he got stuck in an office in Madrid. Listen to Part 1 of the story and answer these questions.

   a Why didn't he notice that everyone had gone home?
   b Why couldn't he get out of the door?
   c Why couldn't he phone for help?
   d Why couldn't he climb out of a window?
   e Why did he want to get into the reception area?

2 Try to imagine how the story ends. Look at the outline below and fill the gaps.

   He noticed a .... on the wall which had lots of .... in it. By the light of .... he managed to find a .... for the .... On the wall there was a list of ...., including the .... He .... him, and he came and ....

   ▭ Now listen to Part 2 of the story, and check your answers.

PRONUNCIATION: Linking words with /w/ or /j/

1 ▭ When one word ends in a vowel sound and the next word begins with a vowel, we often add a /w/ or /j/ sound between them. Listen to these phrases:

Who‿are you?   Tea‿or coffee?
/w/   /j/
No‿oranges   Fly‿away
/w/   /j/

2 ▭ Which of these phrases will be linked with /w/ and which with /j/? Try saying them, then listen.

How interesting   Any others?
So am I   High up in the sky
My uncle   No overtaking
Two or more   Blue eyes

3 Find places in these sentences where words are linked with /w/ or /j/ sounds.

   a They all went to Amsterdam.
   b Who are you talking to on the phone?
   c Go up that way and you'll see it.
   d He isn't very easy to talk to.
   e How many are there? Three or four?

   ▭ Now listen and practise saying the sentences.

READING: Strange – but true?

Australia
In July 1991, residents of the town of Victor Harbour complained that three whales were keeping them awake at night. The whales, which had arrived some days before, had got into the habit of falling asleep near the shore and snoring loudly.

Spain
In December 1990, a postman and his wife were injured when they opened a parcel that he had stolen from work and brought home. The parcel turned out to be a letter-bomb. The postman was later charged with theft.

Indonesia
In January 1991, police arrested a man for selling 'magic pencils' (£225 each) which he said would automatically produce correct answers in university entrance exams. According to the man, the pencils contained electronic signals which would confuse the computers marking the exams and correct wrong answers. Dozens of students complained that the magic hadn't worked for them.

Italy
In March 1990, an Italian American who had emigrated to the USA as a young man in 1948 flew to Italy for the first time in search of his only surviving relative – a great nephew whom he had never met. At his hotel in Rome, he got talking to the barman and explained why he had come – only to discover that the barman was his long-lost great nephew.

Poland
In May 1991, a candidate in a local Polish election decided to vote for his opponent out of politeness – and lost the seat. Out of 595 electors, he was the only one who had bothered to vote.

Great Britain
In August 1987, a Birmingham man was taken to hospital after trying to kill his wife. During the commercial break in a TV programme, he had gone out to the kitchen to make two coffees – one of them poisoned with arsenic. He had then got so involved in the programme (a crime show called *Inspector Morse*) that he had accidentally picked up the wrong cup and drunk it. He was charged with attempted murder.

USA
In 1971, a man went into a bank in Chicago to cash a blank stolen payroll cheque. The thief had made out the cheque to 'Miles F Huml', a name he had picked at random from the telephone directory. He handed the cheque to the bank clerk, who immediately sounded a silent alarm, and the man was arrested. The bank clerk's name was Mrs Miles F Huml. She said later 'I looked at the cheque and I looked at the man, and I knew he wasn't my husband.'

Bangladesh
In April 1991, a baby boy was swept away from a coastal village during a severe storm. He had been given up for dead when rescuers spotted a dolphin holding him in its mouth to keep him clear of the water. The dolphin allowed villagers to take the boy from its jaws. He was later treated for leg injuries caused by the dolphin's grip.

---

1 Here are some remarks that people might make about these eight stories. Which story (or stories) goes best with each one?

   a 'What an amazing coincidence!'
   b 'Extraordinary creatures, aren't they?'
   c 'Some people will believe anything.'
   d 'He got the punishment he deserved.'
   e 'Oh, that was really bad luck!'

2 Six of the stories appeared in newspapers. The other two were made up.
   Which two do you think were made up?

Answer to Question 2

The stories about Italy and Britain were made up. The others appeared in a variety of newspapers. Whether they are actually true, however, is not known.

18 Breaking the law

A Criminals and their crimes

What kind of criminals are these people? Find out by rearranging the letters of their names. Then imagine what each of them did and write a sentence about it.

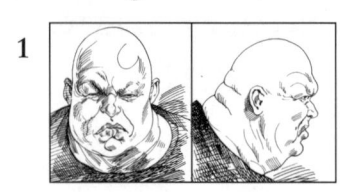

1 Bob Err: **Robber**
He robbed a bank in downtown New York, and got away with $250,000.

2 G Burral: Burglar
She broke into a house and stole a TV set and a video recorder

3 Rich Jake: Hijacker
He hijacked a plane on its way from London to New York and made the pilot fly to Beirut

4 Reg Glums: Smuggler
He smuggled 100 grams of heroin through customs hidden in a tube of toothpaste
  zoll   versteckte

5 Clara Kimble: Blackmailer
She discovered that colleague at work had been to prison, and told him she wanted £2,000 to keep quiet about it.

6 R R Demure: Murderer
Her husband wouldn't give her a divorce, so she pushed him off a cliff.

7 Phil Foster: Shoplifter = Ladendieb
He stole a camera from a department store

8 D V Alan: Vandal
She smashed windows in the local school and sprayed paint on the walls

9 Dan Kipper: Kidnapper
He kidnapped the baby son of a millionaire and demanded a ransom of $500,000

82 *Unit 18* Breaking the law

B Crime story

Fill the gaps in the text with words from the box.

On May 15, 1990, a masked gunman held up a London post office and got away with £5,000. Two days later, Amanda Smith was .... by police and .... with the crime. Three months later, the .... began. The .... claimed that Smith, who was unemployed, had spent £3,000 on new clothes and household appliances on the day after the robbery. They produced .... who said they had seen Smith hanging around the post office for several days before the robbery took place. The .... argued that there was not enough ...., and added that Smith had been in Manchester visiting her sister on the day of the robbery. The .... didn't take long to make up their minds. After only 30 minutes they returned to the court to deliver their ....: Smith was .... The following day, the .... passed sentence: he imposed a .... of £2,000 and sent Smith to .... for two years. As she was led away from the ...., Smith shouted to reporters 'They're wrong. I didn't do it. I'm ....!'

arrest	fine	prison
charge	guilty	prosecution
court	innocent	trial
defence	judge	verdict
evidence	jury	witnesses

New words

Use this space to write down new words from the unit, with your own notes and examples.

TRANSLATION

Translate into your own language:

1 They broke into the office and stole several secret documents.

2 They were arrested for drug smuggling and sentenced to ten years' imprisonment.

3 At the end of the trial, the jury found her 'Not guilty'.

Now cover up the left-hand side, and translate your sentences back into English.

LISTENING: A case of fraud

1 You will hear about a man who thought of a clever way of making money. Before you listen, look these words up in a dictionary.

fraud   generations   family tree
emigrate   greedy   make a fortune

2 Listen to Part 1, and complete what the man wrote in his letters.

a
Dear Mr Thomas,
If you send us ...., we will find out your .... If we find that anyone in your .... was ...., we will send you your ....

b
Dear Mr Thomas,
We are sorry to have to tell you that there is .... in your ....

3 Listen to the second part and find five things that are different from this text:

After a time, he became lazy and stopped sending letters. People in Canada started to complain. They investigated, but they never found the man. The speaker thinks it's a pity he wasn't caught.

PHRASAL VERBS: Prepositional verbs (2)

1 Match these sentences with the the most suitable continuations in the box.

a I *couldn't* possibly *do without* ...
b I *could* really *do with* ...
c The book *deals* mainly *with* ...
d She's taking a long time to *get over* ...
e They're finding it quite hard to *cope with* ...
f Since my illness, I've really *gone off* ...

1 ... greasy food.
2 ... her mother's death.
3 ... my computer.
4 ... bringing up five children.
5 ... the Second World War.
6 ... a long cold drink.

Now listen to the examples.

2 Replace the words in italics with phrasal verbs.

a I really *stopped liking* children after my 5-year-old nephew came to stay.
b He just can't *handle* the pressure of his new job.
c The article *was about* new discoveries in physics.
d He had 'flu, but now he's *recovering from* it.
e I'd *like* someone to help in the office.
f I *really need* a cup of coffee in the morning.

See also the Phrasal verbs reference section on the last page of the book.

WRITING SKILLS: Defining and non-defining relative clauses

1 Look at these pairs of sentences.

A A friend of mine *who lives in Canada* is coming to stay next week.
B My cousin Peter, *who lives in Canada*, is coming to stay next week.

A What's the name of that novel *which became an international best-seller*?
B She wrote a novel called 'Gold', *which became an international best-seller*.

A She's going out with a man *(who) she met on holiday last year*.
B She's going out with a Hungarian called László, *who she met on holiday last year*.

A The place *where I grew up* is a typical seaside town.
B Bournemouth, *where I grew up*, is a typical seaside town.

The A sentences contain 'defining' relative clauses. They define what we are talking about (*Which friend?*, *Which novel?*, *Which man?*, *Which place?*). There are *no commas* before or after the relative clause. Instead of *who* or *which*, we could use *that*:

A friend of mine that lives in Canada is coming to stay next week.
What's the name of that novel that became an international best-seller?

The B sentences contain 'non-defining' relative clauses. They just add more information. There are *commas* before (and after) the relative clause. We cannot use *that* instead of *who* or *which*.

2 Which of these are 'defining' and which are 'non-defining' relative clauses? Mark them *D* or *ND*, and add commas if necessary.

a This is the lever which turns the engine on.
b This is my friend Sarah who I've known for more than 20 years.
c The people who live next door play loud music every evening.
d Is there a shop near here which sells bread?
e Sydney where I lived for ten years is a beautiful city.
f The first car that I ever drove was a Citroën 2CV.

3 Join these ideas to make a paragraph of about seven sentences. Join the sentences with *who*, *which*, *that*, *where* or *and*, and add commas where necessary.

I was sitting in a café. I often go there for a drink after work. I called the waiter. I know him quite well. I asked for a coffee and a ham sandwich. While I was waiting, I looked at a newspaper. It was lying on the table. I started reading an article on the front page. It said, 'Police are looking for a medical student, Veronica Hall. She has been missing from her home for two weeks.' I looked at the photograph. It showed a young woman with dark, curly hair. It was a face. I recognised it at once. She was my new next-door neighbour. She had moved in just two weeks before.

Unit 18 Breaking the law

Review: Units 13–18

1 Sentence rewriting

Rewrite these sentences using the words given.

Example:
They deliver 300 million letters every day.
300 million letters *are delivered every day.*

1 My brother's slightly older than me.
   I'm ....

2 You can't run nearly as fast as me.
   I ....

3 The light switch is too high for my son to reach.
   My son isn't ....

4 The police have recaptured an escaped prisoner.
   An escaped prisoner ....

5 He's not a very good typist.
   .... typing.

6 'They've already gone,' she thought to herself.
   She realised that ....

7 The window was broken.
   Someone ....

2 Verb forms

Write the correct form of the verbs.

Example:
His wallet *was stolen* (steal) while he was standing in a queue at the post office.

1 Now the news. Black's Hotel .... (destroy) by fire. The fire .... (start) in the kitchens last night and quickly .... (spread) to other parts of the building. Rescue workers .... (*still* search) for two missing guests.

2 I .... (try) to lose weight recently. I .... (give) up eating chips and .... (do) a lot of exercise. So far I .... (lose) nearly two kilos.

3 Susan was exhausted. She .... (have) very little sleep the night before, and she .... (*not* eat) anything all day. Quietly, she .... (start) to cry.

3 Vocabulary

1 Match the programmes with the descriptions.

   comedy show   gives you information
   chat show   trying to win prizes
   documentary   never-ending drama
   game show   stars talking about themselves
   soap   makes you laugh

2 What school subject do you associate with

   a dates and battles?   ....
   b maps and climate?   ....
   c poetry and novels?   ....
   d doing calculations?   ....
   e doing experiments?   ....

3 Fill in the missing words.

   I started .... school when I was six, and left .... school at 18. Then I went to university and got a .... in languages. So now I'm a university ....

4 Write in the missing crimes or criminals.

   ....   burglar
   murder   ....
   ....   blackmailer
   vandalism   ....
   ....   robber

5 Match the items on the left with those on the right.

   the accused   give evidence
   the defence   decide on the verdict
   the judge   want a 'guilty' verdict
   the jury   want a 'not guilty' verdict
   the prosecution   the person on trial
   the witnesses   the person in charge

86   Review Units 13–18

4 Fill the gaps

Fill each gap with *one* suitable word. Example:

I ......*was*...... walking through the park yesterday when I suddenly ......*heard*...... a loud scream.

1 The first thing I do when I get my daily .... is to .... to the horoscope. Last Tuesday, it .... me that I .... soon hear from some old friends. Sure enough, I got a phone call from some friends from Australia. They .... just arrived at Heathrow Airport, and said they would .... arriving at my house that evening.

2 I've always .... to learn to play the piano, so recently I've been .... lessons, and I now know .... to read music. I'm not very good .... it yet, but I'm getting .... all the time.

3 Last week I went into a local restaurant to .... lunch. It was terrible. They hadn't cooked the chicken for long ...., and the chips had far too .... salt on them. When I complained .... the waiter, he apologised and explained that he had .... the meal himself, because the chef had .... taken to hospital suffering from food poisoning!

5 Writing paragraphs

Write a short paragraph (2 or 3 sentences) on the following:

1 Which do you prefer, travelling by car or travelling by train? Why?

....
....
....

2 What's your favourite newspaper or magazine? What do you like about it?

....
....
....

3 Think of a story that's in the news at the moment, and write a brief report for a radio news programme.

....
....
....

4 What do you think of the education system in your country? What's good and what's bad about it?

....
....
....

6 Dictation

You will hear a story about a charity shop which sells second-hand clothes.

Listen and write down what you hear.

19 Up to now

A Duration

1 Write out these sentences, choosing between the Present perfect simple and continuous, and between *for* and *since*.

Duration with since & for			
I've She's We've They've	been ill known him been waiting	for since	six months two weeks 1990 September

a I've *known/been knowing* them *for/since* more than 25 years.

....

b He's *learned/been learning* Spanish *for/since* quite a long time.

....

c We've only *had/been having* this video recorder *for/since* Saturday.

....

d They've *played/been playing* cards *for/since* 9 o'clock this morning.

....

2 Now write similar sentences about the people in these newspaper clippings.

a GARY AND EILEEN got engaged in July 1985, the day that Eileen left school – and they're still not married! 'We're not in any hurry,' said

b HARRY PALMER had his first driving lesson on his 17th birthday. Yesterday he was 37, and he spent the morning having his 1205th driving lesson! Yes, Harry still hasn't

c TOM KEMP had a piece of chewing gum in his mouth when he scored the winning goal in the Cup Final two years ago. He decided that it brought him luck, so he kept it – *and pops it into his mouth each time he plays!* 'I won't go onto the pitch without it,' says Tom,

d LAST OCTOBER Ken Garret had an argument with his wife Janet over where they were going to spend Christmas. One thing led to another, and Ken ended up spending the night in the garage. And *he's still there!* 'I told him he couldn't come in until he apologised,' explains Janet, 'and he still hasn't. I wish he would, though. I miss him

a ....
b ....
c ....
d ....

3 Rewrite your last four answers using *since* + clause.

since + clause	
He's been ill (ever) since	he ate that chicken. he arrived. we went swimming.

a ....

b ....

c ....

d ....

88 Unit 19 Up to now

B How long (ago) …?

Imagine that you're going to interview the people below. Ask questions with *How long …?* and *How long ago …?* Use the prompts for the first two people, and make up your own questions for the third.

Example: A novelist
How long ago did you decide to become a writer? (decide to become a writer)
How long have you been writing novels? (write novels)

1 A film star
   How long ago have you been living in B.? (live in Beverly Hills)
   .... (make your first film)

2 The President of IBM
   How long ago did you join the company (join the company)
   How long ago have you been president (be President)

3 The lead guitarist of a band
   How long ago have you been the lead guitarist
   When did you start playing in the band

C Negative duration

Write about three things that you haven't done for some time. Start by saying how long ago it was. The verbs in the box may give you some ideas.

| buy | drink | go | play | see |
| clean | eat | lose | read | write |

Three ways of expressing negative duration

I haven't had a decent meal for three days.

It's a year since I (last) went to the theatre.

The last time I rode a bike was : several years ago.
                                 : when I was a child.
                                 : in 1988.

Examples:

I haven't lost my glasses for at least six weeks. The last time was when I took them off to wash my face at a friend's house, and I left them there in the bathroom.

It's three years since I last went away for a holiday. These days I'm too busy to go away, and I can't afford it either.

The last time I drank sake was when I went to a Japanese restaurant last summer. I remember they served it warm. The meal was wonderful, but it was a bit expensive.

1 ....

2 ....

3 ....

Unit 19 Up to now

TRANSLATION

Translate into your own language:

1 How long has Spain been a member of the European Community?

2 I've known her ever since she first came here five years ago.

3 It must be months since I last wrote a letter to anyone.

Now cover up the left-hand side, and translate your sentences back into English.

LISTENING: Favourite things

1 You will hear three people talking about favourite possessions. Listen and decide which things in the pictures they are describing. Note down words the speakers use that helped.

	Picture	Words
1		
2		
3		

2 Listen again, and answer the questions.

Speaker 1: When was the photo taken?
Who's in the picture?
Why does she like it?

Speaker 2: When and where did he buy the camera?
How did he get the money?

Speaker 3: When and where did he buy the gramophone?
Why does he like it?

PRONUNCIATION: Stress and suffixes

1 Listen to these words on the tape. Notice how the main stress changes.

invite	invitation
imagine	imagination
origin	original
photograph	photographic
national	nationality

2 Look at the words in italics in these sentences. Where is the main stress?

a He loves talking about *politics*.

There are two main *political* parties in Britain.

b We sold our *electric* cooker and bought a gas one.

Here's another bill from the *electricity* company.

c I don't know where he's gone – it's a *mystery*.

Her boyfriend is a rather *mysterious* person.

d The doctor *examined* my ears and nose.

The *examination* starts tomorrow.

e It tastes just like beer, but it contains no *alcohol*.

I'm afraid we don't serve *alcoholic* drinks.

Now listen and practise saying the words.

READING: Four logic puzzles

1 **Five people are waiting to see the doctor.**

Sue came in ten minutes ago.
Richard has been waiting for half an hour – when he arrived, one person was already there.
Tom hasn't seen his friend Ursula for months, so he decided to sit next to her.
Ursula wanted the seat by the window, but it was already occupied.
Quentin broke his arm last week.

Whose turn is it to see the doctor?
What's wrong with Ursula?

2 Maria left school when she was 18, and spent four years at university.
She's been living in the USA ever since she left John.
John's three years older than Maria.
She hasn't seen John since his 30th birthday party.
It's eight years since Maria got her university degree.

How long has Maria been living in the USA?
How old is John?

3 **The inhabitants of the island of Alithia always speak the truth. The inhabitants of the nearby island of Pseudia always lie. Here are some statements made by two married couples, one from each island.**

Alice I'm married to Cecil.
         I've got two more children than Delia.
Brian I've got more than one child.
         I've been married for eight years.
Cecil I've been married for nine years.
         Brian got married a year before I did.
         He's got a son called Edgar.
Delia Alice is a liar.
         She's been married for longer than me.
         She's got four children.

Who is married to whom, and where do they live?
How long has each couple been married?
How many children does each couple have?

	Alithia	Pseudia
names?		
years married?		
how many children?		

4 **Jim, Kate, Laura and Mike often play chess together at the weekends.**
Can you complete the table, using the information below?

The teacher's been playing chess for two years.
The doctor's been playing for twice as long as Jim.
Jim taught the electrician to play a year ago.
Jim learned to play one year after the baker.
Kate always loses to the doctor, but she always beats Jim.
It's one week since the teacher had a game of chess.
In her last game, Laura beat the baker, who's a man.
Mike hasn't played since he lost to the doctor two weeks ago.

	Jim	Kate	Laura	Mike
What is his/her job?				
How long has he/she been playing?				
When did he/she last play?				
Against whom?				
Did he/she win or lose?				

Unit 19 Up to now

20 In your lifetime

A ☐☐☐☐ ☐☐☐☐☐☐ ☐☐ ☐☐☐☐☐

Fill the gaps with words associated with birth, marriage and death. If your answers are right, the letters in circles will spell out the name of the exercise.

I arrived in the world very suddenly. Fortunately, our next door neighbour was a _____, and she rushed round to help with the _____. I was _____ on a Monday night, and my _____ was back on her feet doing the housework by Wednesday morning. A few weeks later I was _____ in the village church …

… In Britain, _____ traditionally wear long white dresses, and get _____ in church. But my _____ was nothing like that. My husband-to-be was not a _____ man, and so the ceremony took place in a registry _____. Afterwards, we had a small _____ in the village hall, and went off on our _____ : a weekend by the seaside …

… In my old _____ I often think about my own death. Should I be _____ in the churchyard, or should I be _____ instead? Will I go to _____ after I die, and what will it be like? And who will come to the _____ ?

B The time of your life

Choose two of the ages in the table, and say what is the best and worst thing about them.

Example:
The best thing about being a baby is that people do everything for you. The worst thing is that you can't talk, so you can't tell people what you want.

The	best / worst	thing about being	a baby / a child / a teenager / in your (20s) / middle-aged / elderly	is …

1 ....

....

....

....

2 ....

....

....

....

C What are they like?

Choose adjectives from the box which best describe these people. Use the pictures to help you.

shy	naughty	rebellious
wise	helpless	independent
lonely	ambitious	self-conscious

1 'He's always stealing sweets, and he pulls people's hair.' ....

2 'By the time she's 30, she wants to be a millionaire.' ....

3 'He knows a lot about the world, and people often ask him for his advice.' ....

4 'She doesn't know anyone – she's got no-one to talk to.' ....

5 'He thinks that everyone is looking at him all the time.' ....

6 'She manages very well without any help from us.' ....

7 'He's a bit scared of meeting new people.' ....

8 'She can't do anything herself – we do everything for her.' ....

9 'Whenever someone tells him what to do he argues about it.' ....

New words

Use this space to write down new words from the unit, with your own notes and examples.

TRANSLATION

Translate into your own language:

1 At a traditional wedding, the guests throw rice over the bride and groom.

....
....
....

2 He was quite shy as a teenager, but now he's become much more self-confident.

....
....
....

3 At what age are you allowed to vote in your country?

....
....

Now cover up the left-hand side, and translate your sentences back into English.

LISTENING: Birth and marriage

You will hear two stories. Story A is about having a baby. Story B is about a wedding.

1 Which of these words do you think will be in Story A and which in Story B, and which can't you be sure about? Mark them A, B or ?

trapeze act	Russians
pregnant	swimming pool
groom	circus tent
midwife	bride
clowns	hospital
pain	reception

Now listen and check your answers.

2 Listen again and complete these sentences.

Story A

a The woman decided to have a baby ...
b The advantage of this is that ...
c She managed to hire a ...
d She also found a good ...
e On May 11, 1985, she ...

Story B

f The man knew a couple who decided to ...
g They invited their friends to come ...
h At the reception, the couple ...
i They had spent a whole week ...

PHRASAL VERBS: Three-word verbs (1)

1 Some phrasal verbs have three parts: a verb, a particle and a preposition. Compare these sentences.

get on   I never visit my sister. We don't *get on*.
get on with   I don't *get on with* my sister.

2 Make three-word verbs by adding phrases from the box to these sentences.

a Your cough will only get better if you *cut down* ...
b I can't stop now – I must *get on* ...
c You can play in the street, but *look out* ...
d She walked quickly to *catch up* ...
e Could you go to the shop? We've *run out* ...

1 ... *for* cars.	4 ... *on* cigarettes.
2 ... *with* the others.	5 ... *with* my work.
3 ... *of* sugar.	

3 Fill each gap with a three-word verb.

a You go ahead. I'll .... you later.
b He's trying to .... meat and eat more vegetables.
c Could you .... the postman? I'm expecting a cheque.
d I don't want to go out. I'd rather stay here and .... my knitting.
e If we don't hurry, we'll .... time.

See also the Phrasal verbs reference section on the last page of the book.

WRITING SKILLS: Joining ideas: showing what's coming next

1 Look at these sentences. Find *one* suitable continuation for each of them in the box.

  a We arrived five minutes before the concert was due to begin. *Surprisingly* ...
  b When I looked in my purse, I realised with a shock that I had no money to pay for the meal. *Fortunately* ...
  c The room they gave me wasn't quite what I'd hoped for. It had a very small single bed, and there was nowhere to hang my clothes. *On the other hand* ...

1 ... most people were already sitting in their seats.	4 ... there was only a washbasin with a single cold tap.
2 ... it was quiet, and I would be able to work without being disturbed.	5 ... there were still very few people in the auditorium.
3 ... the waiter recognised me, and said I could bring in the money tomorrow.	6 ... the manager was very unfriendly, and insisted on taking my name and address.

2 Make sure that you understand the expressions in the box below. Use a dictionary if necessary. Then choose suitable expressions from the box to fill the gaps.

  a Terrorists planted a bomb at Istanbul Airport. ...., it was discovered before it exploded.
  b He entered the room wearing bright red silk pyjamas. ...., everyone stopped talking and stared at him.
  c At first, I didn't like the idea of eating boiled sea snake. ...., it tasted delicious.
  d Diesel vehicles don't have very good acceleration. ...., they're very economical to drive.
  e Pigs aren't as stupid as they look. ...., they're extremely intelligent.
  f I certainly didn't think the film was boring. ...., I really enjoyed it.
  g They were selling all their jackets at half-price. ...., there weren't any left in my size.

> In fact
> On the contrary
> Surprisingly
> Not surprisingly
> Fortunately
> Unfortunately
> On the other hand

3 Write suitable continuations for these sentences:

  a She's certainly not lazy. On the contrary, ...
  ....

  b He went straight up to her and said 'Will you marry me?'. Not surprisingly, ...
  ....

  c Their car got stuck in a snowdrift. Fortunately, ...
  ....

  d The job isn't very well paid. On the other hand, ...
  ....

  e I was hoping to visit the Egyptian Museum while I was in Cairo. Unfortunately, ...
  ....

21 Finding out

A Questions

Write questions beginning *What* and *How*.

1 Has he got black hair? brown hair? blond hair?
 What colour hair has he got?

2 Shall I wear a suit? jeans and a T-shirt? a jacket and tie?
 ....

3 Did it take you 10 minutes to find the house? 20 minutes? 30 minutes?
 ....

4 Do you use *Macleans* toothpaste? *Colgate*? *Crest*?
 ....

5 Do they visit the States every six months? every year? every two years?
 ....

6 Did you have $10 with you? $50? $100?
 ....

7 Do you like mint flavour chewing gum best? strawberry flavour? lemon flavour?
 ....

8 Is your flat one kilometre from the centre? two kilometres? three kilometres?
 ....

B They don't know ...

The police are investigating a murder. The detective's notes tell you what they know so far.

What *don't* they know? Write indirect questions beginning *They don't know* ...

They don't know what time Sir Hugh came downstairs.

....
....
....
....
....
....
....

Indirect questions

Where is he?	→	I don't know where he is.
Has he gone out?	→	I'm not sure if/whether he's gone out (or not).
Why did he go?	→	Do you know why he went?

What we know so far

1 Sir Hugh came downstairs <u>some time</u> during the night.
2 He was typing <u>something</u> when he died.
3 <u>Somehow</u> the murderer knew that he would be there.
4 The murderer hit him with <u>something</u>.
5 Sir Hugh <u>either</u> knew the murderer <u>or</u> he didn't.
6 The murderer has hidden the murder weapon <u>somewhere</u>.
7 The murderer is <u>either</u> still in the house <u>or not</u>.
8 <u>Someone</u> killed Sir Hugh.

C Reported questions

These questions were all asked by the same man on the same day – but who did he ask? Complete each sentence using a reported question.

Reported questions

Where is he?	→	She asked me where he was.
Has he gone out?	→	She asked me if/whether he'd gone out.
Why did he go?	→	She asked me why he'd gone.

Speech bubbles:
- Can I have the day off on Friday?
- Will you pick me up from the office after work?
- Have you cleaned your teeth?
- When is the world going to end?
- When will you be back from lunch?
- How long have you been waiting?
- Did you have a good day at school?
- How much do I have in my account?

1 He asked his 12-year-old daughter *whether she'd had a good day at school.*
2 He asked his wife ....
3 He asked a man at the bus stop ....
4 He asked his secretary ....
5 He asked his bank manager ....
6 He asked his 4-year-old son ....
7 He asked his boss ....
8 He asked a woman with a sandwich board ....

D Question tags

Rewrite these remarks as question tags.

Question tags

It's easy, **isn't it?**	You're not going, **are you?**
He'll come, **won't he?**	She won't mind, **will she?**
You saw it, **didn't you?**	You didn't wait, **did you?**
He's gone, **hasn't he?**	I haven't won, **have I?**

Examples:
I think that's your boss over there. Am I right?
That's your boss over there, isn't it?

In my opinion, that wasn't a very good meal. Do you agree?
That wasn't a very good meal, was it?

1 El Greco wasn't Greek. I don't think so, anyway.
El Greco wasn't Greek, was he?

2 You haven't met the Prime Minister, as far as I know. Or maybe you have.
You haven't met the Prime Minister, have you?

3 I think he was arrested for shoplifting. Is that right?
He was arrested for shoplifting, wasn't he?

4 He's a bit strange, in my opinion. What do you think?
He's a bit strange, isn't he?

5 She's always losing her handbag. Have you noticed that?
She's always losing her handbag, isn't she?

6 Ostriches can't fly. At least I don't think they can.
Ostriches can't fly, can they?

7 I'm sure you won't tell anyone. I hope you won't, anyway.
You won't tell anyone, will you?

TRANSLATION

Translate into your own language:

1 Do you have any idea what time the train leaves?

2 – How long does it take to learn English?
   – That depends on how much you want to learn.

3 – They haven't gone yet, have they?
   – Yes, I think they have, actually.

Now cover up the left-hand side, and translate your sentences back into English.

LISTENING: Phone conversation

1   You will hear one side of a phone conversation. Listen and answer the questions.

- Who is the woman phoning?
- What are they talking about?
- What's the problem?

Now rewind and listen again. What do you think the other person says in the gaps?

a ....

b ....

c ....

d ....

e ....

f ....

g ....

2   Now listen to the whole conversation. How close were you?

PRONUNCIATION: Changing tones

1   Listen to these two-line conversations. Notice the rising and falling tones in the replies. Falling tones are used when we give *new* information; rising tones are used when we *repeat* what has been said before.

a – Did you go abroad this year?
  – I went to New York ↘ in the summer. ↘

b – Did you spend Christmas in New York?
  – No. I went to New York ↗ in the summer. ↘

c – Did you spend the summer in London?
  – No. I went to New York ↘ in the summer. ↗

2 Mark the two parts of the replies with ↘ or ↗.

a – What's Jim doing at university?
  – He's studying French   at university.

b – What's Jim doing now?
  – He's studying French   at university.

c – Are you still engaged?
  – No. We got married   on Saturday.

d – Did you go out yesterday evening?
  – No. I stayed at home   last night.

e – Do you see much of Ian?
  – Oh, I see him   almost every day.

Now listen and practise saying the conversations.

READING: A bit of luck

She put a bunch of flowers on the station bookstall while she opened her purse, and the flowers started sliding towards the edge. I put out a hand to stop them and she gave me a quick, warm smile. Then she picked up her magazine and flowers, and walked away.

And then, when I got on the train, there she was, with an empty seat beside her.

'Anybody sitting here?' I asked.

She looked up from her magazine. 'No, it's all right,' she said.

So I sat there. I wanted to start a conversation, but I didn't know what to say. It was ridiculous. Then I looked at the luggage rack. Her flowers were there. And her small blue suitcase. I read the initials on the suitcase. The letters were Z.Y. Unusual, I thought.

The train started, and as we left the station she stood up and pushed at the window.

'Here, let me help you,' I said. I jumped up and pushed the window open wide.

'I was trying to close it,' she smiled. So of course I apologised and closed the window. And from then on it was easy. We were speaking to each other.

'Going on holiday?' I asked.

'No,' she said. 'I'm just going to spend a few days with my parents.'

'Me too,' I said. 'For a week.'

When the attendant came, I offered her a coffee. 'Thanks,' she said. 'I haven't had a drink since four.'

We talked for a while, and then she stood up and took her things from the rack. I asked her if she was getting out, and she said yes, she had to change trains.

'I hope I'll see you again,' I said.

And she said yes, she hoped so too. And then she was gone. As the train left the station, I suddenly realised how stupid I had been. I hadn't asked her name. I didn't know where she lived. I didn't know where she worked. I could walk about the city for years and never see her again.

And I just *had* to meet her again. But how? What did I know about her? Well, her initials were Z.Y. What name could I make out of that? Zoe Yeadon? Zenobia Yarrow? I had no idea.

When I got back to the city, I looked through the phone book. There were a few pages of Ys, but not one had a Z in front of it.

It seemed hopeless. I thought back. What else did I know about her? She had a case with her initials on it. She also had a bunch of flowers. Flowers!

She couldn't have bought them that morning, because the shops didn't open till nine, and we had caught the 8.50. But wait a minute – there was a flower stall on the west side of the station, and that was open. And to see the stall, she must have approached the station from the west side.

Which buses stopped on the west side of the station? I checked. There were three routes, all of which went to the suburbs of the city. Well, that narrowed it down to a quarter of a million people.

What else did I remember? The bookstall. She had bought a magazine. What magazine? I didn't know. But I did remember the shelf where she had picked it up. I went back to the bookstall and had a look. The *Builder's Gazette*, *Hi-Fi Illustrated*, the *Teacher's Monthly* ... Could she have been a teacher? No – it was a school day when she travelled. The *Electronics Review*, the *Nursing Journal* ... was she a nurse?

And then it hit me. On the train, she said she hadn't had a coffee since four. Four a.m. She'd just come off night duty.

I looked again at the bus routes. One of them passed a hospital. The Royal Infirmary.

I stood in the hospital drive-way, and wondered where I should try first. I saw a door marked *Enquiries*, and was just walking towards it when an ambulance came racing through the gates. I don't know why I didn't get out of the way in time. I just felt the wing hit me, and then I felt nothing more till I woke up in bed saying, 'Where am I?'

'You're in hospital,' said a nurse.

'Is there a nurse here with the initials Z.Y.?'

'That's me,' she said. 'Zena Yates. Why?'

'You can't be,' I said. 'There can't be two people in any one hospital with the initials Z.Y.'

I lay there for hours. Thinking. And then the simple solution struck me. I asked if I could talk to Zena Yates again.

'Yes,' she said, in answer to my question. 'I lent a little weekend case to one of the other nurses. Her name's Valeria Watson.'

And at last she was there, sitting beside my bed, with just a trace of amusement at the corner of her mouth.

'How did you find me?' she asked.

'Luck,' I said, smiling. 'I had a bit of luck.'

Adapted from the short story *Elementary, My Dearest Watson*, by Eric Bean.

1 *a* Where did the writer first meet the woman?
  b What did he realise after she had got off the train?

2 How did these things help the man to find the woman again?
  – flowers?
  – a bookstall/magazine?
  – a cup of coffee?
  – initials on a suitcase?

3 *'Yes,' she said, in answer to my question.*
  What do you think the question was?

4 What was the name of the woman in the train?

22 Speaking personally

A Three ways of talking about feelings

1 Complete the table with the missing forms.

2 Now fill the gaps in these sentences with suitable words from the table.

Verb	I feel ...	I find it ...
annoy	annoyed	annoying
	depressed	
		embarrassing
excite		
	frightened	
relax		
		upsetting
worry		

   a I wish they wouldn't have their TV on so loud. It really *annoys* me.
   b I was just walking out when I realised I hadn't paid the bill. It was really ....
   c Children are often .... of the dark.
   d People often feel .... if they spend too much time just sitting around doing nothing.
   e Why don't you just sit down and .... for a few minutes?
   f The thought of jumping out of a plane with a parachute .... a lot of people, but I love it – it's so incredibly .... !
   g They were very .... when their dog got run over.
   h I hate *karaoke*. I get so .... when I have to stand up and sing in front of everybody.
   i Don't .... ! I'm sure they'll be here soon.
   j I love spending the evening in bed reading a good book. I find it very ....

B A time when ...

Choose two of the topics in the box and say what happened.

Example:
The other day I bumped into another car at a set of traffic lights. Not much damage was done, but the other driver got really angry. He started shouting at me, and I thought he was going to hit me. Eventually I managed to calm him down: I told him that it was all my fault and that I would pay for the damage.

> A time when ...
> ... someone tried to persuade you to do something.
> ... you tried to cheer someone up.
> ... you apologised.
> ... you tried to calm someone down.
> ... you complained about something.
> ... you got angry.

1 ....

2 ....

C Good and bad

These questions all refer to the words in the box. *(sich beziehen)*

positiv		
• awful	entertaining	• amusing
• boring	• fascinating	• terrible
• brilliant	disappointing	• terrific
exciting	• dreadful	• wonderful

threatening · *nasty*

neg: horrible, bad, hateful, naughty, ugly

1 Write down three words that mean 'very good'.
   brilliant
   fascinating
   wonderful

2 Write down three words that mean 'very bad'.
   awful
   dreadful
   terrible

3 What word(s) best describes:

   a a lecture in which you fell asleep?
   a boring novel

   b a TV programme that made you laugh?
   "genial daneben" is very amusing

   c a film that kept you on the edge of your seat?
   The ten commandments were terrific

   d a book that wasn't as good as you thought it would be?
   There were any books disappointing

4 Which word could replace the words in italics?

   'He told me some *extremely interesting* stories.'

New words

Use this space to write down new words from the unit, with your own notes and examples.

New was not one word, but a lot of them I forgot since I went to school.

embarrassed	It's embarrassing to cough in a concert
annoyed	It makes me annoyed, when the staircase is dirty
frightened *(erschreck)*	I feel frightened when it knocks at my door at night
persuade *(überzeugen)*	It hard for me to persuade somebody
conceit *(eingebildet)*	I don't like conceit people
terrify *(erschreckt)*	About the situation in Kiew I get terrify

TRANSLATION

Translate into your own language:

1 He's always complaining about everything. I find it really annoying. ....

2 Why don't you take him out to see a film? That might cheer him up a bit. ....

3 It was a very exciting match. Mendes played absolutely brilliantly, I thought. ....

Now cover up the left-hand side, and translate your sentences back into English.

LISTENING: James Bond films

1 Here are some statements about James Bond films. Which do you agree with? Mark your own opinion in Column A (✓, ✗ or ?).

		A	B
a	They're enjoyable to watch.	✓	
b	They're really exciting.	✓	
c	Sean Connery is a very good actor.	✓	
d	The early films were the best.	✓	
e	They show women in a negative way.		✓
f	The stories and characters are unrealistic.		✓
g	The gadgets and stunts are stupid.		✓

2 🔊 You will hear three people talking about James Bond films. Which opinions does each speaker express? Write *1*, *2* or *3* in Column B. Which speaker do you agree with most?

3 a What does Speaker 1 say that means
   – he's too old for James Bond films?
   – they seem old-fashioned?

  b What does Speaker 2 say that means
   – they have nothing to do with real life?
   – you can forget about everything else?

  c What does Speaker 3 say that means
   – the music in the film was very good?
   – they were very similar to the books?

PHRASAL VERBS: Three-word verbs (2)

1 🔊 Listen to the recording, and complete the three-word verbs you hear.

   a put ....   d look ....
   b look ....   e look ....
   c get ....   f stand ....

2 🔊 Now listen again, and try to guess the meaning of each verb. Write the meaning in your own language. Then use a dictionary to check your answers.

3 Fill the gaps with three-word verbs.

   a Everyone *looks up to* him because he's intelligent.

   b Once I *get down to* writing the letter, I found it quite easy.

   c She *looks down on* everyone who's poorer than herself.

   d My flat *looks out on to* the main square, so it's terribly noisy.

   e It's all we've got to eat, so I'm afraid you'll just have to *put up with* it.

   f She was attacked in the press, but all her colleagues *stood up for* her.

See also the Phrasal verbs reference section on the last page of the book.

WRITING SKILLS: Sequence: unexpected events

1 Look at these pairs of sentences. Which sentence in each pair is about
   – a normal sequence of events?
   – something sudden and unexpected?

   1 a Soon *after* the plane *took off*, they started serving drinks.
     b The plane *had just taken off when* smoke started pouring out of the engine.

   2 a *While* I *was getting* ready for bed, I listened to the news on the radio.
     b I *was just getting* ready for bed when I felt a terrible pain in my chest.

   3 a *Before* he *put* his shoes on, he washed his feet carefully in cold water.
     b He *was just about to put* his shoes on *when* he noticed a scorpion inside one of them.

2 Fill the gaps with suitable expressions, using structures from Part 1.

   a He .... when someone shouted, 'Don't! It's got poison in it!'

   b .... she put the receipt in her pocket and went out.

   c I .... when I suddenly realised I'd left the front door open.

   d .... when the power went off.

   e .... I wiped my shoes carefully on the doormat.

3 Join these sentences to make a story, adding the sentences from the box where you think they fit. Make any changes you think are necessary.

   The telephone rang.

   A voice said, 'Meet me downstairs in ten minutes – it's important.'

   I put my coat on.

   The phone rang again.

   The same voice said, 'Walk straight across the street to the other side.'

   I heard the sound of a car accelerating.

   I ran as fast as I could.

   A Mercedes drove past, missing me by inches.

   > I'd just come home.
   > I was just going out of the door.
   > I was crossing the street.
   > I'd just reached the pavement.

23 The unreal past

A What would you have done?

Would you have behaved in the same way as these people?
What would (or wouldn't) you have done?

Example:

After their picnic, Steve and Janet drove home, leaving their rubbish under a tree.

I wouldn't have left my rubbish lying around. I would have taken it home.

1 After waiting half an hour for the waiter to bring his lunch, Mike just carried on reading his paper.

   If I had waited ½ hour, I would have left the rest.
   I wouldn't have carried on reading my paper
   I would have walked out

2 When Claire's six-year-old son fired his water-pistol at her guests and started pulling their hair, she smiled and said 'He loves playing with grown-ups.'

   I would have told him off (to stop it)

3 An old lady with two large suitcases was taking a long time to get on the train. George was in a hurry, so he pushed her out of the way and got on the train.

4 When Helen got bitten on the leg by a poisonous snake *[giftige Schlange]*, she ran screaming to the nearest village, two kilometres away.

   I would tied a hankerchief tightly round my leg

B Third conditionals *[Bedingungen]*

Complete these sentences.

Example: England would have won the match …
… if they hadn't given away that penalty. *[gesetzl. Strafe]*
… if the referee had been awake.
… if Hodges hadn't been sent off.

> **Third conditionals**
>
> If + Past perfect tense … would(n't) have
> If **I'd known**, I **wouldn't have gone**.
> The play **would have been** much better if the actors **had learned** their lines.

1 I would have bought that painting *if I had had enough money*.
2 If I'd known they were vegetarians *I wouldn't have served Nbg-Bratwürste*
3 *If we hadn't looked to the traficlight* we would have been run over.
4 Your bike wouldn't have been stolen *if you had it locked*.
5 If you hadn't kicked the dog *it wouldn't have bitten you*.
6 *If he had told me lies* I would have smacked him round the face.
7 The party would have been much more fun *if Sam hadn't been there*.

C It's all your fault

The people in the left-hand pictures wish they were in the right-hand pictures, and each thinks it's the other's fault. Write down what each person is saying, using a mixed conditional.

Mixed 2nd and 3rd conditionals

If you'd gone to college, you'd have a good job now.
If you hadn't left school at 15, you wouldn't be unemployed.

If we'd left earlier, we wouldn't be stuck in this traffic jam.
If we hadn't left so late, we'd be on the beach by now.

1 (reserve some seats) *If you'd reserved some seats, we wouldn't be standing in this queue.*

   (get here sooner) .... *we'd be inside the cinema by now.*

2 (pack some blankets) ....

   (fill up with petrol) ....

3 (wear a mask) ....

   (drop the money) ....

4 (bring the right equipment) ....

   (be more careful) ....

D It's all my own fault

Later on, the people in situations 1–4 above stop arguing, and realise that everything was their own fault.

What regrets do you think they might have? Write three or four sentences for each, using *wish* and *should*. You can use the ideas in Exercise C and/or your own ideas.

wish and should

I wish I'd gone to college.
I wish I hadn't left school at 15.

We should have left earlier.
We shouldn't have left so late.

Situation 1
I wish I hadn't arrived so late.
I should have reserved some seats.
I wish I'd gone with someone else.
We should have gone to a restaurant instead.

Situation 2

Situation 3

Situation 4

Unit 23 The unreal past   105

TRANSLATION

Translate into your own language:

1 I certainly wouldn't have invited him if I'd realised what he was really like.

2 – How stupid of me. I should have asked him what his name was.
   – I wish you had.

3 You should have been more careful. Then it would never have happened.

Now cover up the left-hand side, and translate your sentences back into English.

LISTENING: A better place

1 You will hear five people saying what they think would make the world a better place.

   Each speaker uses one word from Column A and one from Column B. Listen and match the words together. Write a sentence showing the connection between them.

A	B
listen	injuries
water	babies
men	exhaust
cars	other people
guns	oil

2 Listen again. Which of these sentences gives the best summary of each speaker's opinion?

   1 a We often don't notice how others are feeling.
     b People are often less happy than we realise.
   2 a Hydro-power is cheaper than oil.
     b We could use the world's resources in a less destructive way.
   3 a Men don't understand enough about small children.
     b By having babies, men would learn to be more caring.
   4 a Exhaust fumes damage the environment.
     b Cars make life dangerous and unpleasant.
   5 a Guns are very destructive.
     b We spend too much money on guns.

PRONUNCIATION: Common suffixes

1 Listen to these common endings.

-al	original, professional
-able	comfortable, suitable
-ous	famous, nervous
-ive	passive, attractive
-ent	violent, convenient
-ment	punishment, argument
-or	actor, survivor
-ion	information, television
-ity	university, electricity
-ful	careful, wonderful
-ture	picture, culture

2 How do you think these words are pronounced?

furniture	invention	engagement
helpful	processor	exhibition
previous	precious	individual
confident	sociable	decision
security	positive	qualification
conscious	official	advertisement

   Now listen and practise saying the words.

READING: If things had been different …

Here are one person's regrets. What can you tell about him? Look at the statements below and write *T* (= True), *F* (= False) or *?* (= can't tell).

a	He and his wife have two children.
b	His wife is Spanish.
c	He lives on the island where he grew up.
d	He speaks Spanish well.
e	He can play the drums.
f	He regrets growing up on a small island.
g	He's never lived outside Europe.
h	He learned Latin at school.
i	He doesn't see his baby during the day.
j	He always does things at the last minute.
k	He's got a piano at home.
l	He's lived in Italy.
m	His wife would like to live abroad.

When I left university, I planned to live in at least five very different countries in at least three different continents. In fact, I only got to live in two, both in Europe, before returning to the UK. Now I'm older, and thoughts of living far away are definitely dreams rather than plans.

I regret the fact that I've always got things done by leaving them until it's nearly too late, and then going mad trying to do it in next to no time. I've learnt to accept that that's the way I am, but I still find I'm always wishing I had done things earlier when there was more time.

I regret giving up the piano about six months after I started learning. My parents told me I would regret it when I was older, but I was about 12, and not bothered by this thought. A few years later, I started playing the drums. I really loved playing them, and became quite good. It would be much easier to have a piano in my house now than a set of drums – they're so impractical and anti-social.

It's a pity that I went to a school where Latin and Greek were not offered as subjects. I've often wanted to know more about the origins of many of the words in English. It would have helped me with other European languages too.

I lived for nearly five years in Spain, but unfortunately I was never in a situation where a Spanish family invited me to their Christmas celebrations, and I've never been to a wedding in Spain. I think Spanish people have a wonderful sense of celebration, and I'm sure these things would have been very enjoyable. Perhaps I should have married a Spanish woman.

I already regret missing so many hours of the first months of my baby's life. He's eight months old now, and I've got used to not seeing him all day, but when he was very small I just wanted to be with him the whole time. I was terrified of missing anything. This feeling began, sadly really, when he was three hours old. My wife had to rest, and there was nothing for me to do but leave them at the hospital and go home.

I wish I'd learned more German during the ten months I spent in Berlin. I found it too easy to make friends who spoke English. I became reasonably good at shopping, and can still remember words for things like 'horseradish'. But now my German's all gone, and I just get confused when I hear it.

I grew up on a fairly small island. I always regretted not living on the 'mainland'. When I first went to the mainland I felt as if I'd seen very little of life compared to everyone else. I used to be amazed by going on trains, or being able to see more than 5 kilometres of land in front of me. Now I don't regret it at all – it means I have a beautiful, peaceful place to visit my parents in every year.

24 Life on Earth

A Environment quiz

Write the answers to questions 1–10 in the diagram. Then read the answer to number 11 (going down).

1. The gradual warming up of the Earth is called '............ warming'.
2. Acid .... destroys trees and kills fish in lakes.
3. The hole in the .... layer may cause an increase in skin cancer.
4. Electricity is produced in .... stations.
5. The waste from this kind of *4* station remains dangerous for hundreds of years.
6. Many factories dump dangerous .... straight into the sea.
7. Burning things releases .... dioxide into the atmosphere.
8. The exhaust fumes from cars and lorries cause serious .... in many cities around the world.
9. A good example of the problem of desertification is the .... Desert.
10. Huge areas of tropical rain .... are disappearing every year.
11. Some gases trap the heat from the Sun in the Earth's atmosphere, making the Earth warmer. This is called the '............ effect'.

B Agree or disagree?

Do you agree or disagree with these statements? Write a sentence or two saying why, or why not.

Example: Factories should pay a 'pollution tax' – the more they pollute the environment, the more they pay.

I think this is a good idea. It would make pollution expensive, and so factories would try to pollute the environment less. Their products would be more expensive at first, but then the price would come down again.

1. Private cars should be banned from city centres.

   ....
   ....
   ....

2. There will never be another accident with a nuclear power station.

   ....
   ....
   ....

3. The size of newspapers should be limited to 20 pages.

   ....
   ....
   ....

C How green are you?

How green are you in your everyday life? Write about the things you do that are good – and bad – for the environment. Use the illustration to help you. (The self-study listening task on page 110 will help too.)

New words

Use this space to write down new words from the unit, with your own notes and examples.

Unit 24 Life on Earth

TRANSLATION

Translate into your own language:

1 They've developed a car that runs on solar power.

2 We need to reduce air pollution by at least ten per cent per year.

3 The orang-utan is an endangered species, and could become extinct within the next 50 years.

Now cover up the left-hand side, and translate your sentences back into English.

LISTENING: How green are you?

You will hear three people answering the question 'How green do you think you are in your everyday life?'

1 Listen and complete the table. (Write ✔, ✘ or ?) Then give each person a score out of 10.

Do they ...	1	2	3
... try to buy 'green' products?			
... try not to waste paper?			
... try not to waste plastic?			
... avoid travelling by car?			
... recycle glass and paper?			
Score:			

2 Listen again and answer the questions.

a What does Speaker 1 say about
  – CFC gases?
  – shopping bags?

b What does Speaker 2 say about
  – brushing his teeth?
  – wearing a jumper?

c What does Speaker 3 say about
  – paper at school?
  – empty cans?

PHRASAL VERBS: Review

1 Match these sentences with the continuations in the box.

a We set off ...
b I'd better get down ...
c I can't work out ...
d I was looking after ...
e Could you pick me up ...
f The café looks out ...
g I could do with ...
h I was in a shop when I ran into ...

| ... to my homework. |
| ... from the station. |
| ... some new clothes. |
| ... the answer. |
| ... on a large lake. |
| ... on our journey. |
| ... an old friend. |
| ... their baby. |

2 Complete these sentences, using a suitable phrasal verb from the box.

a I trusted her, but then she ...
b The plane taxied along the runway and ...
c Give me those letters. I'll ...
d If you run you might ...
e I don't need these shoes. I think I'll ...
f She helps me with everything. I couldn't ...
g She's always complaining. Why do you ...
h Her boyfriend's left her. I hope she ...

| deal with |
| catch up with |
| let down |
| take off |
| get over |
| do without |
| give away |
| put up with |

Now listen and compare what you hear with your own answers.

See also the Phrasal verbs reference section on the last page of the book.

WRITING SKILLS: Organising ideas

1 Look at these paragraphs.

In most parts of the world, typewriters have been replaced by word processors. Word processors allow you to make changes and corrections as you go along. You can also store a text (a business letter, for example), and use it again at a later date.

In most parts of the world, typewriters have been replaced by word processors. The main advantage of word processors is that they allow you to make changes and corrections as you go along. You can also store a text (a business letter, for example), and use it again at a later date.

Frogs and toads, which used to be common throughout the world, are becoming quite rare species. Ponds and marshes are being turned into farmland, and water throughout the world is becoming more acid as a result of air pollution.

Frogs and toads, which used to be very common, are becoming quite rare species. One reason for this is that ponds and marshes are being turned into farmland. But a more important reason is that water throughout the world is becoming more acid as a result of air pollution.

In what way are the second paragraphs clearer than the first?

2 Look at these opening sentences, and choose suitable continuations for each. Start with one of the expressions from the table, and make any other necessary changes.

  a I think the government's plan to build a new city by-pass is very short-sighted. ....

  b It was surprisingly easy for white settlers to occupy land in North America. ....

  c Large dogs aren't very good pets if you live in a small flat. ....

  d I really enjoy speeding along the motorway in my new Porsche. ....

  e I'd much rather be a free-lance journalist than work for a newspaper. ....

One / Another / The / The main / The only	reason (for) / advantage (of) / disadvantage (of) / result (of) / problem (with)	...

Continuations:

The Indians had no sense of private property, so they gave land away or sold it very cheaply.

I can work as much or as little as I want to.

Even more people will travel by car instead of cycling or using public transport.

It uses up an enormous amount of petrol.

They need at least an hour's exercise a day.

3 Choose one of the pairs of sentences. Develop it into a paragraph by adding one or two more sentences.

Review: Units 19–24

1 Sentence rewriting

Rewrite these sentences using the words given.

Example:
They deliver 300 million letters every day.
300 million letters *are delivered every day.*

1 I bought this typewriter when I left school.
  .... since ....

2 They started watching TV four hours ago.
  .... four hours.

3 The volcano hasn't erupted for 500 years.
  It's 500 years ....

4 Where does she live? I've no idea.
  I've no idea ....

5 'Did you lock the front door?' he asked me.
  .... whether ....

6 I didn't have enough money, so I didn't buy it.
  If ....

7 I should have apologised.
  I wish ....

2 Asking questions

Complete the questions.

Example:
– Where *do you work*?
– At Barclays Bank in the High Street. I'm a secretary.

1 – .... learning Chinese?
  – For three years. I'm getting pretty fluent now.

2 – .... my glasses, have you?
  – Yes I have. They're on the shelf in the bathroom.

3 – What .... like?
  – Strawberry, if they've got it. Otherwise, vanilla.

4 – What make .... ?
  – A Volvo. I've only just bought it.

5 – How .... there by bus?
  – About six hours. But it's much quicker by train.

6 – Could you tell me .... ?
  – The station? Yes, it's just up there on the right.

7 – Penguins live .... ?
  – No, they don't. The live at the *South* Pole.

3 Vocabulary

1 What are these words associated with? Mark them
  B (= birth), M (= marriage) or D (= death).

  bridegroom   coffin   midwife
  cemetery   funeral   mourning
  christen   honeymoon   reception

2 Match the items on the left with those on the right.

  ambitious   behaves like a child
  naughty   gets embarrassed easily
  self-conscious   dislikes authority
  rebellious   knows a lot about life
  wise   wants to be Prime Minister

3 How do you think these people are feeling?

  a ....   c ....
  b ....   d ....

4 Find pairs of words in the two columns that have similar meanings.

  entertaining   dreadful
  dull   fascinating
  terrible   boring
  terrific   amusing
  interesting   brilliant

5 Complete these sentences.

  a .... rain kills trees.
  b There's a hole in the ozone ....
  c Scientists are worried about the ....
    effect, which is causing .... warming.
  d As more tropical .... are cut down,
    more endangered species become ....
  e Chernobyl was a nuclear .... station.

4 Fill the gaps

Fill each gap with *one* suitable word. Example:

I ......*was*...... walking through the park yesterday when I suddenly ......*heard*...... a loud scream.

1 It seems strange to me that at 18 I'm .... to join the army and go and .... for my country, but I'm not old .... to go into a bar and buy a drink. I think the .... should be changed.

2 I .... waiting for my bus last night .... a man drove up and asked me .... long I'd .... waiting. I told him I'd only been there .... a few minutes. He then asked if I .... like a lift. When I ...., he began to .... angry, but just then the bus arrived and he drove ....

3 If that asteroid hadn't .... the Earth 65 million years ago, things might .... turned out very differently. Dinosaurs wouldn't have .... extinct, and maybe the .... race would never have evolved. And the Earth would be a .... cleaner place .... it is today.

5 Writing paragraphs

Write a short paragraph (2 or 3 sentences) on the following:

1 Would you rather be a baby, a child, a teenager, an adult, middle-aged or old? Why?

....
....
....

2 Write about a time when you got angry or upset.

....
....
....

3 Think of a film you saw recently. What was it like? Write a short review.

....
....
....

4 What do you think is the most serious environmental problem? What should be done about it?

....
....
....

6 Dictation

You will hear someone talking about a horror film he saw recently.

Listen and write down what you hear.

Review Units 19–24

Tapescripts

Unit 1 Personality types
A Do you like going out to parties?
B Yes, I enjoy parties a lot. I probably go to one party a month perhaps, sometimes more, yes.
A And do you go out to other things like the theatre or the cinema or exhibitions?
B Yes, I regularly go to exhibitions, and I quite often go to the cinema, sometimes the theatre. Opera, quite often, and I enjoy music as well.
A So do you spend much time at home with your family in the evenings? Do you do things with your family at home?
B Yes, I spend a lot of time at home with my family. I have three children, so I spend a lot of time looking after them, helping them with their homework, playing with them, getting them into bed, yeah.
A And do you go out with them much at weekends, say? Do you go out into the country with them?
B Sometimes into the country, although I'm trying to get them interested in things like art, so I take them to art galleries and museums – and they're actually very interested in that.
A Do you ever go camping with them or walking?
B One of them's still rather young for walking. With the older one yes, walking. Camping no, we all find it rather too cold here.
A Do you work at home much? Do you often take work home with you to do at home in the evening?
B Not really. I take the idea of work home, but I never, I never get round to doing work in the evenings, no.
A How many hours do you think you work a day altogether?
B Oh, probably about six hours during the day and very rarely in the evenings.

Unit 2 A Spanish family
Part 1
I used to live with my mother and my sister. And my mother was born just after the war. She belonged to this generation who were brought up thinking that it was the women's responsibility to take the chores in the house and to do the general cleaning, the tidying up, the washing up, the shopping. And if you ask me I think that was precisely her weak point in our education because she didn't give us enough responsibilities, so that we could start doing things on our own like keeping the house tidy, and cooking – I mean we couldn't cook at all. I felt lost once I started living on my own.

Part 2
On the other hand I have two brothers. They're both married professionals and though the men work outside home they also feel that they have the responsibility to take part in the bringing up of their children and so they play with them, they sort of read tales to them and even when they were babies they even changed their nappies. But still their wives are the ones who are mostly at home and they take care of the children. And, well, they do the shopping, they do the tidying up, the washing up, the hoovering, and they even manage the money, the economy of the household. But I think that once the children grow older things will be more equally shared in the house.

Unit 3 Childhood memories
1 I think my earliest childhood memory was when I was nine years old, and I was sent with my sister who was eight to a boarding school. And I remember that – I remember the feelings more than anything. I remember being with my mother and father in the car, and driving up towards this huge, huge house – I've been back since and it isn't that big at all, but obviously I was quite young. And I remember being really frightened about the fact that I was never going to sleep at home again – or so I thought, I mean I did actually go home in the holidays. And I just wanted to burst into tears and cry and say to my mother 'Please, please, please take me home'. But my little sister was crying so much that I had to be a big girl, as my mother would have said, and look after her, and I had to be very brave. And in fact, I had a lovely time there, so it didn't have a sad ending.
2 I think my earliest childhood memory is my first experience of snow, and I've worked out I must have been two, and it was in the mountains, and I can remember having mittens on strings and my mittens froze up and my, what it felt like to have my nose very, very cold and my ears stinging. But I can also remember the sort of bright blue sky and the sunshine – just that it was a very new kind of experience.

Unit 4 A waste of money
A I think things are a waste of money if you buy them simply as a status symbol, if you buy them to show off or you do something in order to, just to show how much money you've got to spend. So things can be a waste of money at times, and at other times they're not a waste of money. So if you go to a very expensive restaurant and have a very expensive meal just to show everybody that you can afford it, and 'Look how rich I am', then I think that's a waste of money. If you buy a very expensive car just because you want everybody to say 'Oh he must be rich' or 'She must be rich' then it's a waste of money. But if you buy, do these things because to you they're special or because they're a treat, and you don't do it extravagantly, you do it because you just enjoy it so much, then I think that's fine.
B I saw an advertisement for a perfume the other day, and the only words on the advertisement were 'The most costly perfume in the world'. Whether it smells wonderful or not, obviously the most important thing here is either for the man to give a woman a very expensive present or for the woman to have it seen on her dressing table. And again it's what you say, it's ostentation, it isn't – I mean, if it smells wonderful then fine, but if it's simply for the expense and to show off then yes, it is a waste of money.

Unit 5 School rules
1 The all-girls school was very strict. The rules – every morning we had to go to prayers, for, it was about half an hour, and we couldn't get out of it, we had to go, otherwise we'd get into trouble if we missed. We had to go to sports twice a week. But it was, I did find it very strict. I had to wear a uniform in the school – that was very strict as well. We had to wear a navy skirt which had to be a certain length. Quite a lot of people tried to have them a bit shorter, but that wasn't allowed.
2 There were certain rules, you know, that don't apply at the sixth-form college, like we weren't allowed to go out at all during the day, during lunchtime or break or anything, we had to stay in college. We weren't allowed into the classrooms or anything, so even during winter it was very cold out. And I thought those, I don't know I thought some of the rules were stupid like that. (What about uniform?) Did you have to wear a uniform?) Yeah, yeah we did. I mean, I don't mind wearing uniforms you know. I find it a lot easier than having to get up every morning and decide what to wear, so I didn't mind that. It wasn't a very nice uniform, mind you.
3 It was a private school, a girls' school, and I think probably the strictest thing about it was the uniform, which was just completely ridiculous. It was grey, white and pink. The skirt had to come, you know, exactly two inches below your knees, the socks and like even the buttons were like regulation school buttons. In lesson time it was, you know, absolutely no talking. Everyone sat at separate desks in very straight rows. And it was, you know, needlework was compulsory, we had handwriting lessons. I mean, exactly the kind of education that thankfully

that we're kind of moving away from now, i.e. just learning facts and then regurgitating them in an exam.

Unit 6 Going home
Part 1
At the end of the holiday, we took everyone to the airport and left them to check in, you know, for their various flights. And one group – I think it was about five men in their mid-twenties – were going to Manchester. They found their plane was overbooked and that there wasn't any room for them, so they came to see me and I tried to find room for them on another flight. But they were all full, so I could only get them onto a flight for the following afternoon. I mean I told them that they could get money back from the company and I'd arrange free food and drink for them at the airport. Anyway one of the men was starting a new job the next day and they weren't very happy and they all started complaining and suddenly the man with the new job went crazy, he started shouting, and suddenly he put his hands round my throat and started shaking me around.

Part 2
Within about, well, just a few seconds about eight security guards surrounded them and pointed guns at them. The man, you know, stopped immediately. I tried to calm things down and said, you know, there was no problem, but they arrested him and took him away. Well I went too and after about half an hour I managed to persuade them there was no harm done and they released the man. Two policemen went with him and sat with the group until they boarded their plane. I managed to get him onto a London flight and he caught a train up to Manchester and would you believe he got to his new job on time.

Unit 6 Phrasal verbs
1 If you carry on working like that you'll make yourself ill.
2 I grew up in a large house in the country.
3 We've got a long way to drive, so we ought to set off as early as possible.
4 Oh dear – I've just found out that I've only got £10 in the bank.
5 They invited lots of people to the party, but hardly anyone turned up.
6 Don't ask me to share an office with Debbie – we don't get on at all.
7 Now you're 30 it's time you settled down and got a good, steady job.

Unit 7 Changed lives
1 Well I used to be a sales rep for the company I work for now, and of course it meant I travelled all over the place, all round the country, and I went to Europe quite a lot as well, which was wonderful – I really enjoyed it at the time, but it was very tiring. And then I got promotion, and now I'm a manager for my local area, so it means I stay at home. Most of the time I go home at the end of every working day. And I really like it – it means I've been able to make my home look very nice and work on the garden – so it's great.
2 Well up until a couple of years ago I was still single and I had quite a busy social life – I used to go out almost every night and I was pretty exhausted most of the time. But now I'm married and got a small baby, and I stay in a lot more than I used to. Mind you, I'm just as exhausted, because the baby keeps us awake at night.
3 I used to work as a production assistant in a television company, and it was a fairly glamorous job. I travelled a lot, I got to eat at great restaurants and stay in nice hotels, and my friends were all pretty envious. But they didn't realise the pressure that I was constantly under and the tension that existed, you know, every day. So I decided to change jobs and I work for a national charity now that provides guidance to troubled children, and I really, really enjoy it.

Unit 8 On the phone
1 A Hello, dental surgery.
　B Hello. Is there any chance of an appointment today? It's a bit of an emergency.
　A Could you tell me exactly what the problem is?
　B Yeah, I've broken a filling, and it's really, really uncomfortable.
　A Well, let me see. Mr Jones is very busy but he might be able to fit you in about 5 o'clock this afternoon. Is that any good?
　B Any earlier?
　A If he came back from lunch early – yes, 1.30.
　B Oh, that'd be great, yes.
　A Could I take your name, please?
　B Yes, it's Davie.
　A Right. Well, thank you Mrs Davie. See you at 1.30. Goodbye.
2 A Ace Photography.
　B Oh hello, I wondered if you could help me. I need – I don't know if you do this – I need a passport photograph.
　A Passport photos, yes we do. (Yeah) Yes we do.
　B Would it be very expensive?
　A Well, we do four passport photos in a group for £11.50.
　B £11.50. Oh that's quite good. I wondered if you could fit me in at all?
　A Well, yes of course. If you just pop by, it takes about two minutes to take the photograph, and they should be ready for you within about a quarter of an hour.
　B Right, that's wonderful. So just pop by?
　A Yes, at your convenience. (Great, I'll do that) We're open until half past five.
　B Thanks a lot.
　A Bye.
3 A Hello, Fred's Motors.
　B Oh hello, it's Mrs Williams here. I'm just phoning up because my Volvo is making very, very strange noises, and I wondered if you'd be able to have a look at it.
　A Yeah. When was the last time you had it serviced?
　B I think it was only about a month ago. But it's a sort of knocking noise.
　A Well bring it in, bring it in tomorrow morning, yeah?
　B Tomorrow morning. About what time?
　A About 8.30. Is that all right?
　B Right that's lovely. Thank you very much. Goodbye.

Unit 8 Phrasal verbs
1 Could you turn it up? I can't hear what he's saying.
2 Don't forget to switch it off when you go out.
3 I'll have to look it up in my dictionary – I'm not sure what it means.
4 Don't throw them away – you can recycle them.
5 Let's ring them up and see if they want to come with us.
6 I'd better take them off – they're soaking wet.
7 Turn it off – the water's overflowing.
8 Why don't you try them on and see if they're strong enough for you?
9 Let's sort them out and see which ones we really want to keep.

Unit 9 What would you do?
Would you give a lift to a hitch-hiker at night?
1 If I was on my own, absolutely not. If my husband was with me, well I don't think so either, no I wouldn't.
2 Yes I, yes I would, as long as there was somebody in the car with me at the time of picking up the hitch-hiker – yes.

Would you give money to a beggar in the street?
1 That would depend. If I thought that person was just begging money to buy alcohol or something, I don't think I would. But if it was a sincere homeless person, or perhaps a single mother on her own, then I might think twice about it and give her some money, yes.
2 If I had enough money, I think I would. But I think I would look before I actually gave the money, and check, first of all that it was a beggar. (Yes) And also that perhaps if there's a group of people begging, that I've got enough money to give something to everybody.

Would you ever cheat in an examination?
1 No I would never ever cheat in an examination. What's the point of taking an examination if you're going

to cheat in it? It wouldn't mean anything.
2 I'd like to say no, that I wouldn't, but I think if I could manage to do it without being caught, I'd do it, yeah.

Would you ever drive a car after drinking alcohol?
1 I must admit in my youth to having done it once or twice. But no, now I would never do it, since I've learned, you know, the problems and how dangerous it is.
2 Personally I wouldn't, because I don't drink anyway, but I think it's OK to have one glass or two glasses – I think you're fine. I think it's just when someone's had too many drinks and then they start driving – that's dangerous. (Yes) But personally no, I wouldn't.

Would you give up your seat on a bus for an elderly person?
1 Yes, I would give up my seat. Actually, the sign says 'Don't sit', you know, or 'Give up your seat if an elderly person or somebody with children wants to sit here', so I try not to actually sit in those seats.
2 Oh I, yeah, I'd do that, yeah. I think that's being respectful to the older generation.

And lastly, would you kill someone in self-defence?
1 If I thought my life was truly being threatened, that if I didn't kill I would be killed, yes I would.
2 Yes, I'm pretty sure I would, if it meant defending my own life, protecting myself. I'd do anything to protect my own life, I'm pretty sure. And yes, I would kill, yeah.

Unit 10 Things for sale

1 A Hello. The Pearson residence.
  B Oh hello. I was ringing up about the advertisement in the paper for an electric cooker. Is that you?
  A Yes, it is. We still have it for sale.
  B Oh good. How old is it?
  A Well, it's about five or six years old. (Uh huh) It has two ovens (Uh huh) and four burners and it's in very good condition.
  B Are you still using it?
  A No, we're not using it any more because we've bought a gas cooker. (Ah) Would you like to come and take a look at it?
  B Yes, I think so. Where are you, actually?
2 A Hello. 770606.
  B Hello. Is that the person who's advertising the wooden desk?
  A Oh yes, yes, that's right, yeah, that's me. (In the paper)
  B You've still got it, have you? (Yeah, yeah) What sort of desk is it?
  A Well, it's a bit of an antique, actually, used to belong to my grandad. It's got, well obviously a fold-out bit at the top which you can write in, and it's got three drawers underneath. It's quite interesting.
  B And what's it made of? What's the wood?
  A I'm not a great expert at wood, actually, but I think it's got some sort of veneer over the top which looks like walnut. I don't know if it is. (Really?) It is old.
  B And you're selling it for £60?
  A Yeah, or near offer, yeah.
  B Yeah. OK, well can I come and see it?
  A Yeah. It's a bit difficult today, but are you free tomorrow any time?
  B Yeah, in the morning I could come.
  A Morning, fine, yeah. What time would suit you?
  B About nine o'clock.
  A Right, OK, nine o'clock. (OK) What's your name, sorry?

Unit 10 Phrasal verbs

1 A What's 53 times 115? I can't work it out.
  B Why don't you use a calculator?
2 A Peter wants me to go on holiday with him.
  B Will you go?
  A I don't know yet – I'll have to think it over.
3 A We can't get enough people to play in the match on Saturday.
  B Oh dear. We'll have to put it off till next week, then.
4 A That's a lovely song. Who's it by?
  B Me – I made it up myself.
5 A Coffee?
  B No thanks, I'm trying to give it up. It's bad for my heart.
6 A I didn't know you went jogging.
  B Yes, I took it up a few weeks ago – it's really good.

Unit 11 When I'm 60 ...

I think that by the time I'm around about 60 I will probably be surrounded by children. I have visions of me sitting out on a large verandah, possibly in Australia, and looking out across the garden, and the garden being absolutely immense, and me having designed most of it, planted most of it, and probably lived in most of it for a few years. By that time I imagine that I will have travelled through most of Europe, I think that I will speak two languages apart from English fluently, I certainly hope so. I think that I'm going to be a person who's going to be very active, I think that even when I'm 85 I'll be in the garden, I think that when I'm 65 I'll still be skiing. I think that that would be my goal, actually, I think for me to be able to go skiing where I wanted to when I wanted to, to have some feeling of family with lots of children and a big house and friends. But I think that I will have probably met somebody that I liked enough to live with without killing them and that hopefully we'll sort of settle down for the end of our lives together. I think that that would be my ultimate dream, it would be a nice way of finishing my life.

Unit 12 Narrow escapes

Story A
Well I was probably about five years old and we lived in a large block of flats with a big garden at the back, and a lot of us children would play out there. And one day I was out there, and there was a boy who was a bit older than me who was chopping wood with an axe. And I came up behind him without him seeing me, and as he swung the axe back it went through my – just below my lip, and there was a lot of blood. And I ran home screaming, and the doctor came and stitched it up, and fortunately it's only a very tiny scar, but it could have been very nasty indeed.

Story B
A girlfriend and I were living in a trailer up in the mountains, and it wasn't actually the right kind of trailer to be up the mountain, you know it wasn't strong enough. And there was a horrendous blizzard one night, one of the worst blizzards of the century, and it dumped a lot of snow everywhere. And the next morning we tried to get out the front door of the trailer, and it wouldn't budge, and when we opened up, tried to pull the curtains back to call for help – the snow was completely covering the window, so nobody could hear us or anything. We thought it was kind of funny and were giggling a bit, but you start to get a little bit nervous. And the mountain rescue team had to dig through like ten feet of snow on top of the trailer to get to us, and they were convinced that we had, you know, suffocated from lack of oxygen. We were just real glad to see them.

Unit 13 Living in Britain

1 The thing that I find very annoying is separate taps for cold and hot water, because when you haven't got any plug at hand and you want to wash your hands, you simply, you know, either boil your hands using the tap for hot water or you turn your hands into two pieces of ice using the other one. And another thing is left-hand-side driving which makes driving impossible for me because I really can't change gears with my left hand. And I also find it very difficult to cross the street because I always feel very surprised seeing the car coming from the direction which I really don't expect it to come.
2 What is quite different, I think so, is how polite English people are compared to French people. Just, for example, when you're in the street and then you just suddenly bump into someone and the way people say 'Oh I'm really sorry, excuse me, dear'. Or even when you're queueing

somewhere, the English people just go in the queue and just wait for, they just wait quietly and don't say anything.
3 I think that the strangest thing that I've noticed, especially lately, is that people have an attitude here to possibly the way you speak and definitely the way that you dress. For example, I was in town the other day, it was a very, very sunny day and I'd just finished work and I went for a swim and when I was walking home I was walking in my cut-off shorts and I had no shoes and socks and a towel and a T-shirt and the amount of people that stared at me as if they'd never seen a pair of shorts before or somebody with no shoes and socks before, struck me as strange.

Unit 14 Media habits

1 A What newspaper do you read mostly?
B I read *The Scotsman*, which is, I think, Scotland's biggest national newspaper. I like it because it's very interesting for local news, but at the same time it has very good coverage of other British news items, and it's good for international news as well.
A Do you read any weekly magazines?
B Um yes, I read *The Economist*, which is closely associated with my work.
A What about television? What do you watch on television?
B Well unfortunately I don't watch very much television. I find I don't really have enough time for that. And in fact I spend a lot more time listening to the radio, I think really because I find I can do other things at the same time as listening to the radio. On the radio I always listen to the news, probably two or even three times a day, and news discussion programmes.
2 A What newspapers do you read?
B Well I buy *The Times* because it's got a really good crossword, and I can't get through the day without the *Times* crossword.
A Do you read any weekly magazines?
B Yes I get the magazine called the *New Scientist,* which is essentially about news in science around the world, and that's just because I'm interested in science generally.
A What about television? What do you watch on television?
B I like watching movies, especially if they're thrillers or detective movies, that kind of thing, where I can just sit down for the evening and relax.
A Do you listen to the radio at all?
B Yeah, all the time, even when I'm working. Again I prefer talking radio rather than just music, music, music. And I find that I can work and listen to the radio at the same time.

Unit 14 Phrasal verbs

1 He gave all his money away.
2 He gave away the plans to the enemy.
3 The music's too loud – could you turn it down?
4 They offered him the job, but he turned it down.
5 His parents brought him up much too strictly.
6 I decided to bring up the question of pay at the meeting.
7 I looked up Botswana in the atlas.
8 You must look me up if you're ever in London.
9 Pick up that bag – you dropped it.
10 I'll pick you up at 5.30 and we'll go there together.
11 They've put up a huge block of flats near the station.
12 You don't need to stay in a hotel – we can put you up for the night.

Unit 15 What has happened?

1 A Karl, it was a really good party last night. (Thanks) Terrific. But look, I've lost one of my earrings.
B Oh no, you're joking. Where?
A Well, I'm not sure, it could be anywhere. (Um) It looks like a blue dolphin.
B Right, well, do you know which room you spent most time in last night?
A No, anywhere really.
B Well, did you dance?
A Yes, (Right) a lot.
B OK, well you probably lost it there. I tell you what, I'll have a look in the lounge, and then I'll ring you back, yeah?
A Oh thanks a lot.
B All right.
2 A Hi Sue, it's me.
B How did you get on?
A I've passed.
B Oh Chris, that's brilliant news.
A Oh God, yeah, I'm so pleased, it's such a relief.
B Third time lucky, eh?
A Third time lucky. I wasn't sure I was going to do it at all, but ah, I'm so relieved …
B What was the examiner like?
A He was really nice actually. He made me feel really relaxed early on. And I didn't really have any problems.
B What about your parking and your reversing?
A No that was all fine. I was just so much more relaxed this time.
B Oh, you must feel over the moon.
A Yeah, as a celebration, I'm going to take you out for a drive over the weekend. What do you reckon? (Oh superb)
3 A Listen, I've got a real problem.
B What is it?
A The car's broken down.
B Oh not again.
A Yeah, I checked the oil, and I checked the battery. It's not, I don't know what it is, it's just not starting at all.
B You'll have to get rid of it you know.
A I know, I know. But look, the thing is, I've got to pick Samantha up at the airport.
B Do want to borrow mine?
A Do you mind? (No) I know I'm covered by the insurance.
B Well you drove it last week, didn't you?
A Well, that would be a great favour.
B Oh, come round when you like. I don't need it till tonight.
A OK, I'll be round in about an hour. (OK) Thanks a lot.

Unit 16 Three school subjects

1 I think my most tedious memory at school was at biology when we had to learn the Latin names of lots of plants and animals, and we'd spend hours looking at them written down on the blackboard and just having to copy them out and remember them. Seemed a real waste of time to me.
2 History was great fun. We didn't have to learn dates – well we had to learn some of course, yes, but we didn't get good or bad marks for knowing or not knowing history. We learned a lot about individuals, famous people, not so famous people, it seemed to all make sense and it felt as if history had a meaning for us. No, it was great, it was good, I enjoyed it and the teachers seemed to make it very realistic and true to life.
3 Well, one of the subjects that I learned at school was history, which I felt very critical about the way that I learned it, because we learned a lot about kings and queens and battles and emperors and things. We never actually really learned that much about people and their everyday lives, and how they survived, how they made a living, how they survived through these wars.
4 Science was not very well taught. It wasn't the fault of the teachers, rather that they didn't have the money to supply the equipment that you need. We just didn't have that. What the teacher would have to do was stand at the front of the class and perform the experiment himself, and we'd just have to watch, we wouldn't have the chance to actually do the experiment ourselves, which would have helped us learn.

Unit 17 Locked in!

Part 1
I went down to Madrid to work for a month for a big company down there, and it was my first Friday, I'd only been there a few days, and they'd cleared out an old storeroom and put a desk in it for me and I was working away and it must have been about five o'clock in the

evening when I walked out of my little office, and I realised that everybody had gone home. And the main lights were all out, so I ran downstairs in case I could catch somebody leaving but it was too late, the doors were all locked, and I was stuck. So I ran upstairs again and picked up the phone, one of the phones, and it was dead, so I tried another phone and that phone was dead as well, and clearly they'd switched the phones off for the weekend. So I went to the window and the windows wouldn't open, they were barred, and it was beginning to get dark, and I thought 'Well, I'm here for the weekend.' Anyway, what I did eventually was I went downstairs again to the reception area and the reception was a small room with glass walls and of course it was locked but I noticed that inside there was a phone which had a little red light on it.

Part 2
And there was a cabinet up on the wall in the hallway which was locked of course but it was full of keys. And somehow I managed to break this open and inside there were hundreds of keys, and I thought 'Well one of them must be the key to this reception area', and I had a box of matches with me fortunately because it was getting really dark now, this was January, and I tried key after key after key and eventually I found a key which fitted this reception area. And I went inside, and there was a list on the wall of a number of phone numbers including the duty officer. And this phone was in fact live, and I picked it up and called this man, and he was pretty cross because he was just going off to the opera I think, but he came round in his dinner jacket and let me out, and so I got home.

Unit 18 A case of fraud

Part 1
I know of an amazing case where a man was charged with fraud. What he'd been doing was, he'd got some headed paper from the British Government and had written to countries like Australia and Canada and South Africa where he knew that a lot of people from England had emigrated and he said in this letter 'We the British Government, if you send us $10, or £10, will trace your lineage and find out your family tree and if we find that anybody in your family going back over the generations was famous or of interest, we will let you know and send you your family tree. A lot of people received this letter and obviously thought 'Well that's interesting' and they sent him $10. And a few months later he would send them a letter back saying 'There's nothing of interest in your family tree.' And they did nothing about it.

Part 2
But he got away with this for a long time but eventually he became greedy and sent so many letters out that it became impossible to answer all the letters, and people started to complain about it and as more and more complaints occurred in each country they started to investigate and discovered this man who had made a fortune out of it. And I think it was rather a shame that he was caught because I think for $10 it's a story worth being involved in really and I think, you know, he only ever took $10 at a time from each person, and I think he deserved to keep it.

Unit 18 Phrasal verbs

a I couldn't possibly do without my computer – I use it all the time.
b I'm dying of thirst – I could really do with a long, cold drink.
c The book deals mainly with the Second World War, but there are some chapters on life in the 1930s.
d She's taking a long time to get over her mother's death – they were very close to each other.
e They're finding it quite hard to cope with bringing up five children – they're thinking of getting a childminder.
f Since my illness, I've really gone off greasy food – even the smell of it makes me feel sick.

Unit 19 Favourite things

1 One of my favourite things is a photograph of my sister and me. It was taken about ten years ago when we were both very young, standing on the beach in our shorts and T-shirt, and it was a very sunny day and we both look very happy in the photograph. And I like to keep this photograph because it's a nice memory and I can look back and remember the fun we used to have when we were younger. So it's something I'd like to keep always.
2 One of my favourite possessions is my camera. I often go out and take photographs. I bought it when I was much younger, about 12 years old, in New York in a second-hand shop. I can remember saving up my money for at least a year beforehand and choosing it very carefully in the window. I use it quite often to go out and take photographs. It's not one of the most expensive cameras that you can buy, and it might now seem quite outdated, but very often what's more important for making nice pictures is your own eye and judgment of the situation rather than how much it costs.
3 One of my favourite things is my wind-up gramophone, you know one of the ones with the big horn. I got that about, oh, seven or eight years ago in Malaysia. I'd been looking for one for a long time in this country, but they're terribly expensive. But I was working in Malaysia, and I found one there in a sort of antique shop, and it was just affordable, so I bought it there. And not only is it a very, I think, beautiful object in its own right, but it also brings back very strong memories of Malaysia for me. And I listen to it quite regularly and I often go out looking for old gramophone records to play on it.

Unit 20 Birth and marriage

Story A
When I was pregnant with my first baby, I read an article in a magazine about having a baby in water. And it was the Russians I think who first decided that this was a good idea, because it said in the paper you didn't feel any pain. So I actually decided that this is what I'd like to do. So I went and looked, tried to find somewhere because, you know, you can't go to your local swimming pool or anything, so I found this company and they hire out these fantastic little swimming pools. And then the difficulty was to find a doctor or a midwife or someone like that who would actually let me give birth to my baby under water. And I found this really, really lovely midwife and I've stayed friends with her ever since. And on the 11th May 1985 my little girl was born, and we never even went near a hospital – it was wonderful.

Story B
A couple of years ago I went to an extraordinary wedding. These two friends of mine tried to think of something different, and what they did was they decided to get married in a circus, so they got married in this circus tent, and invited all their friends to come as – they didn't want anyone to be dressed formally so they, we all went in fancy dress, as gangsters, as whatever, some people went as clowns, obviously, it being a circus. But what was even more extraordinary was when we got to the circus, for the reception, there was the church service and then we went off to the reception in the circus tent, what none of us knew was that the bride and groom had rehearsed for a whole week this trapeze act, and they were going to do it in front of all of us at the beginning of the wedding. So they came on, and did this incredible trapeze act, which I think was one of the most extraordinary weddings I've ever been to.

Unit 21 Phone conversation

A Hello? Hello, is that Mr King? This is Julie Richards.
B Ah yes, you're phoning about the printer, aren't you?
A Yes that's right. Have you had a look at it yet?
B Yes, we have. I'm afraid the motor's burnt out.
A Oh dear. Will you be able to repair it, do you think?
B Oh no, we couldn't repair it. We'd have to put in a new motor.

A I see. And how much would that cost?
B That would be let me see, £245 including labour.
A Oh, that sounds an awful lot. How much would it cost to buy a new printer?
B A new printer would be £320.
A Oh really? It's hardly worth repairing then, is it?
B Well, it isn't really. You might as well get a new one, yeah.
A OK, I think I'll probably have to do that, then.
B Right. Would you like to order one now from us?
A Um, well I'm not sure. I'll think about it. OK, thanks anyway. Bye.

Unit 22 James Bond films

1 I used to find them quite exciting and amusing, but I think I've grown out of them now. They seem a little bit outdated. For example the gadgets they use in them – they were supposed to be the latest inventions and now they seem ridiculous to our generation. And for example you realise that the stunts they use in the films are very artificial and also the situations in which they put the characters, they're quite forced. But apart from those negative points I think they could be quite enjoyable for some people.
2 I really enjoy James Bond films because they're very exciting and I like all the gadgets that they have and because they're pure escapism, you can really just switch off and enjoy watching them and enjoy the adventure of it. And although I suppose they're very sexist as well, somehow it seems to be OK because they're James Bond films, and it doesn't matter too much.
3 I love them, especially the early ones. *From Russia with Love,* a brilliant film, brilliant theme music, and Sean Connery was a terrific actor in his role as James Bond. And the beauty of the early films was that they followed the books pretty closely. And I had read all of the James Bond novels and so it was very interesting to go and compare of course. And I loved the earlier James Bond, but the later ones not so much. They became more like comedies. I think a lot of people found them entertaining because of that but I didn't like the later ones as much as I liked the earlier ones.

Unit 22 Phrasal verbs

a He always comes home after midnight. I don't know why she puts up with it.
b It's a nice quiet room. It looks out on a small garden.
c Well, it's time to get down to some work. It's nearly 10 o'clock.
d He was a great leader and the whole country looked up to him.
e Just because he hasn't got a job is no reason to look down on him.
f You ought to stand up for yourself. Don't let them tell you what to do.

Unit 23 A better place

1 I think the world would be a better place if everyone listened to each other a bit more. I think we go through life not listening, not taking any notice of how other people are feeling, and how things are upsetting them or if they're happy.
2 I think the world would be a better place if there were, there was no oil to be used for power. The world is seven tenths water. Therefore, those seven tenths water could quite easily make hydro-power. It would be cheaper, it would be cleaner, it would be using the world's resources and raw materials in a positive way, not just burning them and getting rid of them and creating more poison.
3 I think the world would be a better place if men had babies for a change, and they suddenly had to have a whole new kind of experience. It would be very interesting to see how the world might change and improve if they were responsible for the care of babies and families.
4 I think the world would be a much better place if we didn't have so many cars on the road, and also if the speed limit was dropped as well. But it's also the exhaust, the fumes, it's just getting overcrowded, it's just not pleasant to go out for a walk any more.
5 Well I think the world would be a better place if there weren't any guns. Just look at how much they cost and look at the cost in human lives and in injuries and so on caused only because of guns. Yes, no guns.

Unit 24 How green are you?

1 (So how green do you think you are in your everyday life?) I think I do the basic, you know, necessities, I think for example when I go shopping I don't buy products if they've got CFC gases, and I always make sure that they haven't been tested on animals. I think I probably could do a lot more, for example I tend to use paper, I'm not conscious of how much paper I'm using and I know I probably waste a lot. I do drive a car, but that has unleaded petrol in it. Another thing is plastic I think, I'm not conscious of how much plastic I, you know, for example in the supermarkets I don't take my own shopping bags, I tend to use more and more bags each week, and I think that's bad. So I think basically I do as much as I can for myself but if I really made an effort I could do more.
2 (How green do you think you are in your everyday life?) In my everyday life I think I am green. I don't run the tap while I'm brushing my teeth. I will sort out rubbish and take bottles to the bottle bank, paper to the paper bank, etc. But I'm very hypocritical in that I do a lot of driving, and often it's unnecessary driving, in that I'm polluting the atmosphere with the fumes from my vehicle. I'm green from the point of view that I use two sides of a piece of paper. I don't waste paper – I use both sides if I have to. However I do turn the heating up and waste electricity as opposed to putting an extra jumper on.
3 (How green do you think you are in your everyday life?) Well we certainly use green products, I suppose you'd have to call them, around the house, you know, recycled loo paper, recycled kitchen roll, recycled plastic bottles, and we certainly make an effort to recycle anything that we can, like glass jars or glass bottles. In school we have a recycling paper system which I do try and stick to. There's a tray in every classroom, and instead of throwing away paper into a wastepaper-basket you just put the paper in there and it's recycled and collected every week. I'm not as green as I could be, I think, in the way that I'm quite lazy – if I have a can, you know, which is empty I will throw it in a bin, I won't take it home with me and save it up, you know. But we don't have a car, which is I think a big thing – we all cycle, which is really good. Always take our own shopping bags when we go shopping, which I think we did even before the big green thing came along, you know, for convenience as much as anything else.

Unit 24 Phrasal verbs

a I trusted her, but then she let me down.
b The plane taxied along the runway and took off.
c Give me those letters. I'll deal with them.
d If you run you might catch up with them.
e I don't need these shoes. I think I'll give them away.
f She helps me with everything – I couldn't do without her.
g She's always complaining. Why do you put up with her?
h Her boyfriend's left her. I hope she gets over it soon.

Answer key

Unit 1 Regular events

A Explanations

2 Vegetarians don't eat meat.
3 In Switzerland, most people speak German.
4 Roman Catholic priests don't get married.
5 She doesn't have a job. (She hasn't got a job.)
6 British drivers drive on the left of the road.
7 The President of the USA lives in the White House.
8 The sun rises in the east.
9 He doesn't know how to read and write.
10 Banks don't open on New Year's Day.

C Present simple passive

Ice-cream: They're eaten by Hollywood stars. The finest ingredients are used.
Shoes: They're made from real leather. They're designed for your comfort. They're guaranteed for 12 months.
Story-books: They're used by all the best schools. They're written by experts. They're illustrated in full colour.

D At the moment

Possible answers:
1 … They're doing all the washing, and they're painting the children's bedroom.
2 … People are lying in the parks and sunbathing. Everyone's eating ice-cream. Lots of people are sitting outside in the sun.
3 … I'm spending the whole day in bed, and I'm watching a lot of TV. I'm reading lots of magazines, and everyone's bringing me fresh fruit to eat.

Listening: Personality types

1 a ✓   b ✓   c ✗   d ✓   e ✗   f ✗
2 *Possible answers:*
   A sociable type   5–7
   A culture-vulture   7–9
   A home-lover   6–7
   An outdoor type   2–3
   A workaholic   1

Pronunciation: The sound /ə/

2 a Russian tractor
  a million dollars
  a famous conductor
  a colour photograph
  the Argentinian Government
3 a I'm reading a brilliant American novel.
  b My sister's attending a conference in London.
  c Will you answer the question?
  d Fortunately the driver wasn't injured in the accident.
  e My cousin's picture is in today's newspaper.

Reading: How to saw someone in half

1 1C; 2G; 3E; 4B; 5A; 6F; 7D

Unit 2 Around the house

A Good housekeeping

Across: 3 where 4 lying 5 switch 8 used 9 mess
11 keep 12 use 16 leave 17 late
Down: 1 clean 2 away 6 wash 7 tidy 9 makes
10 she 13 clear 14 water 15 meal

B Labour-saving devices

b microwave oven   f vacuum cleaner / hoover
c (electric) drill   g washing machine
d iron   h dishwasher
e (electric) cooker

C Features of rooms

Possible answers:
1 a bookshelf; a sofa; a coffee table.
2 There's patterned wallpaper on the walls. There's a painting hanging on the wall, and a mirror. The floor is bare floorboards. There's a thick rug on the floor.
3 Two vases; some (framed) photos; some plants; a statue.
4 There's a view of the sea and a modern city.
5 The room looks quite elegant, but comfortable, too. Maybe it needs a couple of comfortable chairs as well as the sofa. The decoration is quite tasteful.

Listening: A Spanish family

1 just after; traditional; did all the housework herself; unable.
2 a B   c B   e M
  b B   d W   f W

Phrasal verbs: Introduction

2 a be careful   d visit
  b find the meaning of   e raise your head
  c have a view of   f try to find

Writing skills: Punctuation: joining sentences

2 *Suggested answers:*
  a [:]   d [–]
  b [because]   e [:] ; [, and]
  c [, so]
3 *Possible answer:*
  Our new range of kitchen tables comes in three exciting colours: pale green, lemon yellow and fiery red. The tables are made of tough plastic – they're almost impossible to scratch or burn, and the surface is easy to wipe clean after your meal. Just fill in the

form below and send it to us, and then sit back and relax – we'll deliver the table to you within a week. You can pay in any way you like: in cash, by cheque or by credit card. If you're not completely delighted with your table, you can send it back, and you won't owe us a penny.

Unit 3 Past events

A Short stories

Possible answers:
2 I was driving along the main street ... so I had to walk home.
3 ... when he slipped. The food went all down the front of my shirt ...
4 I was walking home late one night ... I said 'No' and he just ran off.
5 ... when it suddenly ran off into some trees. It came back five minutes later with a rabbit in its mouth.
6 I was cooking my dinner last night ... so I had to give them something to eat too.

B Subject and object questions

1 Who won seven Olympic gold meals in 1972?
  How many gold medals did Mark Spitz win in the 1972 Olympic games?
2 Who married Richard Burton twice?
  How many times did Elizabeth Taylor marry Richard Burton?
3 When did the Americans land on the moon?
  What happened on 20 July 1969?

D Active or passive?

... began ... stole ... was arrested (was caught) ... was released ... met ... robbed ... were often killed ... were offered ... were chased ... always escaped ... were caught ... was hit ... were killed.

Listening: Childhood memories

1 a 1   c 2   e 2
  b 2   d 1   f 1
2 1 nine years; a boarding school; frightened; sleep at home; cry (burst into tears); crying
  2 two; snow; froze up; very, very cold; ears; bright blue sky; sunshine

Pronunciation: Reduced and full forms

2 a some /ə/   d some   g do /ə/
  b to   e was /ə/
  c for   f was

Reading: Two terrible tales

Holiday in New York
2 H; 3 B; 4 G; 5 C; 6 F; 7 A; 8 D
The bed by the window
2 D; 3 E; 4 A; 5 I; 6 G; 7 H; 8 C; 9 B

Unit 4 Money

A Using money

1 Do you accept credit cards?
2 How much do these ties cost?
  I'll have these two, please.
  Could I have a receipt, please?
3 Can I cash some traveller's cheques, please?
  Where do I sign them?
4 Could you give me change for this £10 note?
  Is there a bank near here?

B The (6) of living

1 rent   3 price   5 bank   7 bills   9 life
2 tax   4 spent   6 cost   8 save   10 expensive

C Similar meanings

1 I can't afford (to buy) it.
2 It's a waste of money.
3 It doesn't cost much. (It doesn't cost a lot.)
4 Can you lend me £5?
5 He owes his parents more than $1,000.
6 He earns £800 a week.
7 He paid $500 for that jacket.

Listening: A waste of money

2 b
3 a to show people that they can afford it.
  b they want people to know they're rich.
  c to give them a very expensive present.
  d so that people will see it on their dressing table.

Phrasal verbs: Intransitive verbs (1)

1 set off – arrive   take off – land
  get up – go to bed   come in – go out
  wake up – go to sleep   get on – get off
  stand up – sit down   speed up – slow down
2 a take off   f set off
  b get up   g getting off
  c woke up   h sat down
  d Stand up   i slow down
  e Come in

Writing skills: Reference: pronouns

1 a coat; her coat; your coat; Peter's coat
  b a cot; our cot
  c some money; any money
  d tulips; the tulips
2 a ... – it's *yours*.
  b ... you can borrow *mine*.
  c ... Have you got any bigger *ones*?
  d ... or a small *one*.
  e ... hadn't got *any*.
3 I sat down and waited. Eventually a waiter appeared and I ordered onion soup. After a long time, he brought me *some*, and then I noticed that my spoon was dirty. I asked for another *one*. After another long wait, he brought me a clean *one*, but *it* was much too

Answer key   121

small, so I asked if I could have a bigger *one*. After about ten minutes, he brought me *one* that was clean and the right size. Then I noticed that there wasn't any bread, so I called the waiter again and asked him for *some*. He told me there wasn't *any*.

I finished, paid the bill and asked for my coat. The waiter brought *one* that I didn't recognise at all. I told him it wasn't *mine*, and that *mine* was a black leather *one*. He came back with a brown jacket.

'Is this *yours*?' he asked.

Unit 5 Obligation

A Obligation structures

1 don't have to / don't need to
2 Do I have to / Do I need to; can
3 aren't allowed to; have to / need to
4 have to; can't / aren't allowed to
5 can / are allowed to
6 can I / am I allowed to; have to

B Make and let

They don't let him have long hair.
They make him run six kilometres a day.
They let him go home one weekend a month.
They don't make him wear uniform on his days off.
They don't let him complain about the food.

Listening: School rules

1 *a* 3; Yes   *c* 1; Yes   *e* No-one   *g* 2; No
   b No-one   *d* 1; Yes   *f* 2; No
2 *a* 1   *b* 3   *c* 2

Pronunciation: Contracted forms

1 She will; He would; You are; I have not; They had; It is not; We have
2 *a* I *don't* have any change, *I'm* afraid.
   b *They're* sure they *haven't* seen him.
   c *He'll* come if he *isn't* busy.
   d *I've* been to Athens, but he *hasn't*.
   e *You'd* better look where *you're* going.
   f I *can't* hear the music – *it's* too quiet.

Unit 6 On holiday

A Holiday activities

Possible answers:
Scottish Highlands: We climbed several mountains, including Ben Nevis. We carried all our food and equipment in backpacks, and at night we camped in a small tent and cooked our own food. One night it was so wet that we stayed in a hotel, and had haggis, which is a Scottish speciality.
Italy: Every night we stayed in a different city. We visited Florence and went to several art galleries and museums. In Rome we did a lot of sightseeing, including, of course, the Colosseum. And we brought back a lot of souvenirs – one was a model of the Leaning Tower of Pisa.

Florida: We stayed in a hotel right on the beach, and spent most of our time swimming, sailing and waterskiing. And we went on two excursions: one to Disney World, and one to Florida Keys.

B Holiday puzzle

1 boat; train; car; bus; plane
2 package; camping
3 passport; tickets
4 cathedral; castle
5 sandals; shorts
6 beach
7 sail; windsurf; swim
8 ski; skate
9 picnic; barbecue
10 compass; map
11 souvenir; camera

```
S B E N A L P F A B E
T O C A M E R A D U X
E A R I N E V U O S T
K T W I N D S U R F S
C S A P A C K A G E S
I R W K S A I L N H A
T R O P S S A P I C P
O S H O R T S C P A M
S A N D A L S H M E O
E N E U C E B R A B C
L A R D E H T A C J Y
```

Listening: Going home

1 *a* 2   *c* 1   *e* 3   *g* 4
   b 6   *d* 8   *f* 7   *h* 5
2 Eight security guards surrounded them.
  They pointed guns at them.
  I tried to calm things down.
  They arrested the man
  Later they released him.
  I got him a seat on a London flight.
  He got to his new job on time.

Phrasal verbs: Intransitive verbs (2)

2 *a* found out   *e* carried on
   b grew up   *f* turned up
   c didn't get on   *g* settled down
   d set off

Writing skills: Subject and object relative clauses

2 I had quite a good time in Cambridge, although *the family I stayed with* was rather boring – they spent a lot of time watching TV and didn't go out much. Fortunately, *the people who lived next door* were very friendly, so I spent a lot of time with them. Also, *the school I studied at* organised trips at the weekends, so I went to quite a lot of interesting places. I'm sending you some photos of *a place we visited on an excursion*. It's just a small town, but it's got *a cathedral which was built in the 11th century*. The person in the foreground is *a girl I met at a party* – her name's Véronique.

3 This is a photo of ...
  a ... some students who were in my class
  b ... a building (which) I could see from my bedroom window.
  c ... the person who taught us English.
  d ... a party (which) we organised at the end of term.
  e ... the train (which) I came home on.

Review Units 1–6

1 Sentence rewriting

1 He goes abroad (once) every three months.
2 My brother always does the washing up.
3 I met them during my/the summer holiday.
4 *The Godfather* was written by Mario Puzo.
5 Could/Would you lend me your car?
6 We aren't allowed to go to bed / stay up late.
7 They made me stay in / inside / in the house.

2 Asking questions

1 How often do you eat out?
2 How many children have you/they got?
3 What was the weather like?
4 What was he doing when you arrived?
5 Who gave it to you? / Who did you get it from?
6 Could you change this £5 note? / Could you give me change for this ... / Have you got change for this ...
7 Do I have/need to wear a suit? (Must I wear a suit?)

3 Vocabulary

1 culture-vulture – visiting art galleries
  outdoor type – going for walks
  sociable type – going to parties
  workaholic – doing overtime
2 *a* drill
  b fridge/refrigerator
  c vacuum cleaner / hoover
  d washing machine
3 riot – people are arrested
  earthquake – the ground shakes
  war – cities are shelled
  flood – people drown
4 *a* rent   *c* bill
  b tax   *d* insurance
5 souvenirs – shops
  local specialities – restaurants
  excursions – buses
  windsurfing – water
  sightseeing – fine buildings

4 Fill the gaps

1 leaves; puts/tidies/clears; mess; off; tap/water; up
2 value; waste; afford
3 uniform; what/whatever/anything; don't/never; let

6 Dictation

The idea of going on holiday is to relax. You don't have to do any housework, you can go to bed and get up whenever you like, and you can spend the day swimming, skiing, sunbathing or doing whatever else you want. Unfortunately, things don't always turn out like that.

Last winter, for example, we went on an expensive skiing holiday. The plane was delayed for nine hours, and we arrived at the resort a day late. The next day, someone crashed into me on the mountain and broke my shoulder, and I had to spend the rest of the week in hospital.

In the summer we went on a package holiday to Florida, and that wasn't much better. Our luggage was sent to the wrong airport, and took three days to reach us. Then our hotel room was broken into, and our passports and credit cards were stolen, along with our traveller's cheques and return tickets. So we spent the next few days sitting at a desk in a police station, instead of lying by the hotel pool.

Next year I think we'll spend our holidays at home. It's safer, cheaper and you don't have to pack a suitcase. And it's much more relaxing.

Unit 7 Past and present

A Used to

1 We *used to work* long hours, but we *didn't use to get* much pay.
2 There *used to be* a cinema near my house. I *used to go* there every Saturday.
3 – How *did* you *use to get* to school?
   – I *used to walk*. And when I was older, I *used to cycle*.
4 There *didn't use to be* much traffic in those days. We *used to play* football in the street.

B T h i n g s h a v e c h a n g e d

... s*t*opped ... *th*rown ... *j*oined ... lear*nt* ... *g*iven ... lo*s*t ... bou*gh*t ... *ha*d ... s*h*aved ... applie*d*

... *c*losed ... taug*h*t ... *p*aid ... resig*n*ed ... *ch*anged ... gon*e* ... starte*d*

C How have they changed?

Possible answers:

1 ... She used to travel all over the world. She's got a job as a waitress. People don't recognise her any more. She used to be very rich.
2 They used to work in the city. She used to be a secretary. He used to wear a suit. They've retired. He doesn't have to wear a suit any more. They don't have to get up in the morning.
3 He didn't use to have any money. He used to be a beggar. He's become very rich. He doesn't sleep on the street any more.

D Present perfect passive

2 The clothes have been washed.
3 The candlestick has been polished.
4 The cup has been mended.
5 The concert has been cancelled.
6 The letters have been opened.
7 The cat has been fed.

Listening: Changed lives

1 *Speaker 1*: sales rep; manager
   Speaker 2: single; married; a small baby
   Speaker 3: production assistant; television company; changed jobs; charity
2 *a* 1, 3   *c* 1   *e* 3
   b 1, 2   *d* 1, 2 *f* 1, 3

Pronunciation: Syllables and stress

1 1 *syllable*: cars, picked
   2 *syllables*: murder, murdered, published
   3 *syllables*: murderer, photograph, magazine, library, understand, religious
   4 *syllables*: international
3 *a* studying – architecture – University
   b interviewed – President – television
   c another – photograph – grandparents
   d journalist – newspaper
   e understand – complicated

Reading: Two childhoods

a J	*e* PJ	*i* ✗	*m* P
b P	*f* P	*j* PJ	*n* J
c J	*g* P	*k* J	
d J	*h* J	*l* PJ	

Unit 8 At your service

A Having things done

1 photographer's; garage / service station; laundry / dry cleaner's; dentist's; hairdresser's; optician's
2 *Possible answers*:
   b I had my photo taken.
   c I had my car serviced.
   d I had my coat cleaned.
   e I had a tooth filled.
   f I had my hair cut.
   g I had my eyes tested.

B How do you do it?

1 borrow; card; member; join; form
2 receiver; coins; dial; dial; international code; local area code
3 parcel; post office; weigh; stamps; registered

Listening: On the phone

1 Davie; a broken filling; 1.30
2 photographer's; passport photo; four; £11.50; two minutes; 15 minutes; 5.30
3 A *woman* phones the garage because her *Volvo* is making a strange *knocking* noise. She last had it serviced about a *month* ago. She arranges to take it into the garage at 8.30 *tomorrow morning*.

Phrasal verbs: Transitive verbs (1)

2 1 turn up the TV / the TV up
   2 switch off the light / the light off
   3 look up the word 'pronoun' / the word 'pronoun' up
   4 throw away your empty bottles / your empty bottles away
   5 ring up your friends / your friends up
   6 take off my boots / my boots off
   7 turn off the tap / the tap off
   8 try on these glasses / these glasses on
   9 sort out our holiday photos / our holiday photos out

Writing skills: Punctuation: direct speech

1 *a* Capital letter for a new sentence; no capital letter when it's a continuation of a sentence.
   b The full stop comes first; commas come first too.
2 *a* 'I'm hungry,' he said. 'Is there anything to eat?'
   b 'Don't go yet,' he begged her. 'Stay a little longer.'
   c He asked me quietly, 'Do you know why I'm here?'
   d I said, 'Here's the money I owe you.'
   e 'I may be poor,' he said, 'but I'm not stupid.'
3 There was a ring at the door. I went to open it and found an old woman standing outside.
   'I'm sorry to trouble you, sir,' she said, 'but I'm collecting old clothes to sell. Have you got anything you can give me?'
   'Wait a minute,' I told her, and went into the bedroom. I found an old jumper and a pair of shoes, and went back to the front door. The woman looked taller and younger than before, and she was pointing a gun at me.
   'Don't move,' she said, 'or I'll shoot.'

Unit 9 Imagining

A Would and wouldn't

Possible answers:
1 … they'd be very frightened.
   … it would probably upset their boat.
2 … they wouldn't notice.
   … they'd have to walk home.
3 … they wouldn't be very pleased.
   … they'd make him tidy the place up.
4 … it would probably attack the people.
   … they'd soon stop laughing.
5 … the drinks would go all over the guests.
   … they'd have to go home and change.

B Second conditionals

Possible answers:
1 … if he ironed his clothes.
2 … I'd keep it.
3 If the Government put up taxes …
4 … if I lived nearer the office.
5 … you'd spend more time with me.
6 If I was/were the President …
7 … if I had a nice place to live.

C Wishes

1 I wish it would stop raining. / I wish it wasn't raining.
 I wish we had a car.
 I wish there was a café near here.
2 I wish I spoke (could speak) French.
 I wish someone would speak to me.
 I wish I knew someone here.
3 I wish I lived somewhere quieter.
 I wish I could go to sleep.
 I wish they'd close the motorway at night.

Listening: What would you do?

1

	1	2
hitch-hiker	✗	✓
beggar	✓	✓
examination	✗	✓
alcohol	✗	✗
seat	✓	✓
self-defence	✓	✓

2 *a* Neither   *e* Both
  b 1   *f* 2
  c 2   *g* Neither
  d Both

Pronunciation: Linking words: consonant + vowel

3 *a* The books are on the table in the corner.
 b It's a waste of money to buy lots of clothes.
 c I drink at least a litre of milk every day.
 d Wake up and put your clothes on – they've arrived.
 e My sister and I are about the same height.
 f Small igloos take just over an hour to build.

Reading: My perfect weekend

1 *1* i   *4* g   *7* a   *10* b   *13* o
   2 n   *5* k   *8* e   *11* m   *14* j
   3 h   *6* c   *9* l   *12* d   *15* f

2 mosquito; squid; backgammon; goats; octopus
3 *a* False. She's taking a large sunhat; she's waiting till late afternoon before swimming.
 b True. She knows all about it – even the room over the fish shop.
 c False. She's leaving the other tourists on the other island; she wouldn't welcome a busload of tourists.
 d True. 'At least 20 new Greek words.'
 e True. She'd leave behind her alarm clock, word-processor and phone.

Unit 10 Describing things

A Identifying objects

1 *a* drill, 10   *f* map, 2
  b souvenir, 6   *g* plug, 7
  c receipt, 1   *h* stapler, 5
  d nappy, 4   *i* disk, 9
  e razor, 8   *j* typewriter, 3

2 *Possible answers:*
 a A tool for knocking nails into wood.
 b A brush you use for cleaning your teeth.
 c A small piece of metal you use for locking and unlocking doors.

B Compound nouns

1 di*sh*was*h*er   7 *f*ootball b*oo*ts
2 *a*larm clock   8 wra*pp*ing *p*aper
3 dri*v*ing glo*v*es   9 r*ai*nc*oa*t
4 pencil sharp*en*er   10 *d*riving mi*rr*or
5 *t*oo*t*hpas*t*e   11 ligh*t* swi*t*ch
6 shop *w*indo*w*   12 *s*ungla*ss*es

Compound nouns *have two parts.*

Listening: Things for sale

1 *Possible answer:*
 For sale. Electric cooker. Five years old. Two ovens. Four burners. Very good condition.
2 *a* True   *d* False
  b False   *e* False
  c False
 Picture C

Phrasal verbs: Transitive verbs (2)

1 work it out – a maths problem
 think it over – a suggestion
 put it off – a football match
 made it up – a song
 give it up – coffee
 took it up – jogging
2 *a* give up   *d* work out
  b taken up   *e* think (it) over
  c put (it) off   *f* made up

Writing skills: Reference: *this* and *which*

2 *a* which   *c* This
  b it   *d* which
3 *Possible answers:*
 a Many new cars have power steering, which makes them much easier to park.
 b Parking is limited to two hours in the city centre. This encourages people to go to work by bus.
 c In 1812, Napoleon decided to invade Russia, which turned out to be a serious mistake.
 d In Luxor you can hire a horse-drawn carriage, which is a very romantic way to see the town.
 e At the age of 18 I won £100,000. This completely changed my life.
 f Most yachts have compartments filled with air, which makes it almost impossible for them to sink.

Unit 11 The future

A Optimism and pessimism

Possible answers:

1 The weather will probably be warm and dry.
 It'll rain.
2 We'll leave on time.
 The plane will probably be delayed.
3 I'll probably land on nice, soft ground.
 I'll probably break both of my legs.
4 They won't look inside my socks.
 They'll probably search me.

B Expect and hope

Possible answers:
1 I hope the weather's warm and dry.
  I expect it'll rain.
2 I expect we'll leave on time.
  I hope the plane isn't delayed.
3 I hope I land on nice, soft ground.
  I expect I'll break both of my legs.
4 I don't expect they'll look inside my socks.
  I hope they don't search me.

C Will be doing and will have done

Possible answer:
Oil will have run out, and everyone will be driving electric cars. Millions of people will be living on the Moon, and people will even have landed on Mars. The world's population will have reached 20 billion. The quality of life will be better: scientists will have found a cure for the common cold, and people will only be working an average of 20 weeks a year. Most families will be taking seven holidays a year, and underwater holidays will be the most popular.

D Giving reasons

Possible answers:
1 ... Otherwise, I'll be tired in the morning.
2 ... in case you lose it.
3 ... because it'll get very cold at night.
4 ... Otherwise they won't know you're coming.
5 ... so that you wake up on time.
6 ... in case there's a power cut.
7 ... because they might not accept credit cards.
8 ... so that you don't forget it.

Listening: When I'm 60 ...

1 *a* False   *c* False   *e* True
  b True   *d* False   *f* True
2 verandah; garden; designed; settled down; children; active; skiing

Pronunciation: Stress in sentences

2 *a* – Where's my bag?
     – On the table.
  b – What's the time?
     – Five past six.
  c – What are you doing on Saturday?
     – I'm going to a party.
  d – Are you ready?
     – I'll come in a minute.
  e – Where's the butter?
     – It's in the fridge.
  f – What nationality is he?
     – I think he's Greek.
  g – What does he look like?
     – He's got a beard.

Reading: Crossing the Sahara

1 *a* You might tread on a scorpion or a horned viper.
  b There might be a scorpion in it.
2 If you break down, you can't walk to safety.
3 *a* Stay.
  b Drink it, say goodbye and leave.
4 *b*, *d* and *e* are good advice.

Unit 12 Accidents

A Bad luck

Possible answers:
1 ... She fell over and twisted her ankle.
2 He was skiing down a hill when he hit a tree and broke his leg.
3 The baby was playing with some matches when she set the carpet on fire and burnt her hand.
4 She was mending the light when she touched a live wire and got an electric shock.
5 He was cutting vegetables when the knife slipped and he cut his hand.
6 While she was eating peanuts, one got stuck in her throat and she nearly choked.

B Dos and don'ts

Possible answers:
1 Put cushions behind the person's head and under his knees. Loosen clothing around the neck. Don't give him anything to eat or drink.
2 Block the gap under the door with wet towels. Open the window and call for help. Don't open the door.
3 Tie something above the bite. Make a cut and suck out the poison. Don't walk around.

C On the road

1 skid   6 brake
2 indicate   7 run over
3 crash   8 accelerate
4 fault   9 overtake
5 swerve   10 insurance

Listening: Narrow escapes

Story A
a He was chopping wood with an axe.
b She came up behind him.
c Just below the lip.
d She ran home screaming.
e The doctor stitched it up.

Story B
a There was a blizzard.
b It was blocked with snow.
c The window was blocked with snow, so no-one could hear them.
d They thought it was funny, but they felt nervous.
e Dug through the snow to the trailer.
f They thought the people inside would be dead (from lack of oxygen).

Phrasal verbs: Transitive verbs (3)

1 a 5 d 4
  b 2 e 6
  c 1 f 3

2 a ran it over   d put me down
  b knocked him out   e talk him round
  c make her out   f let me down

Writing skills: Joining ideas: clauses and phrases

2 a Although he knew Chinese ...
  b ... in spite of her age.
  c ... because of the bad weather.
  d ... except that he hasn't got any/much experience.
  e ... because of the risk of catching malaria.

3 *Possible answers:*
  a We decided to go camping in spite of the bad weather, and we had a wonderful time.
  b I enjoy living in Cairo, apart from the noise and the traffic jams.
  c Although she had good qualifications, she wasn't given the job because of her age.
  d Although it was Saturday evening, the café was completely empty, except for a couple at a corner table.

Review Units 7–12

1 Sentence rewriting

1 I don't live in Canada any longer.
2 A new bypass has been opened.
3 I had my TV repaired last week.
4 I wish we had a video camera.
5 Tipp-Ex is used for correcting typing mistakes.
  or Tipp-Ex is used to correct typing mistakes.
6 I don't expect they'll arrive on time.
7 Leave early in case the roads are crowded.

2 Verb forms

1 Have you written; posted
2 used to be (*or* was); he's grown
3 had
4 wouldn't like
5 could
6 will be punished
7 we'll have finished; we'll be lying

3 Vocabulary

1 a at a garage or service station
  b at an optician's
  c at an electrician's
2 dial – a number
  fill in – a customs form
  join – a library
  lift – the receiver
  wrap – a parcel
3 a lifting a car wheel off the ground
  b eating Chinese/Japanese food
  c weighing yourself
  d removing a nail from a piece of wood

4 a a carving knife
  b a frying pan
  c an address book
  d a filing cabinet
  e (a roll of) toilet paper
5 accelerate – to go faster
  brake – to slow down
  overtake – a slow-moving vehicle
  run over – a pedestrian
  skid – on an icy road
  swerve – to avoid hitting someone

4 Fill the gaps

1 if; bit; move/walk; so; had; out
2 stuff; made; on; called
3 have; flying/going; might/may; hope
4 narrow; while; fell/dropped; set; smoke/flames; brigade

6 Dictation

My part of town used to be a pleasant place to live. The main street was full of shops, all owned by local people, and I could get everything I needed simply by walking down the road.

Now they've opened one of these large shopping centres right on the edge of town. There's a huge supermarket, an American toy store, a vast store selling electrical goods, and a film centre showing 15 different films at once.

The result is that the local shops are going out of business. The fish shop and the electrician's have closed, and the local cinema will have closed by the end of the year. Pretty soon they'll all have gone, and I'll have a 20-minute drive to buy a loaf of bread.

The problem is that people don't think. They go rushing off in their cars to save five pence on a bag of potatoes, and forget that it has cost them £2 in petrol to get there. If they thought about it, they'd leave their cars at home and go shopping locally instead. And then maybe some of the local businesses would survive. But I don't expect for one moment that it will happen.

Unit 13 Comparing and evaluating

A Small and big differences

1 Cars aren't nearly as dangerous as motorbikes.
2 CDs are slightly more expensive than cassettes.
3 English is much more useful than Greek.
4 French mustard isn't quite as hot as German mustard.
5 The train doesn't take quite as long as the bus.
6 His qualifications aren't nearly as good as mine.

B Comparison of adjectives and adverbs

Adj	good	*AA*	fast
Adv	well	*Adv*	clearly
Adj	friendly	*Adj*	comfortable
AA	hard	*Adj*	funny

1 better
2 better
3 more friendly / friendlier
4 harder
5 faster
6 better/more clearly
7 more comfortable
8 funnier/better

C Too and enough

1 He was too heavy.
  The chair wasn't strong enough.
2 It was too difficult (for him).
  His Spanish wasn't good enough.
3 It was too high (for him to climb).
  He wasn't fit enough.
4 There were too many questions.
  He didn't have enough time.

Listening: Living in Britain

1 separate taps – wash your hands
  cross the street – seeing the car coming
  bump into someone – 'Oh, I'm really sorry'
  left-hand-side driving – change gears
  walking in my shorts – people stared
2 *Speaker 1*
  a The water is either too hot or too cold when she washes her hands.
  b Because the gear stick is on the left.
  c Surprised.
  Speaker 2
  a Polite.
  b They wait quietly.
  Speaker 3
  a Cut-off shorts and a T-shirt.
  b Shoes and socks.
  c They thought he looked unusual.

Pronunciation: Linking words: consonant + consonant

2 a Is it good luck to see a black cat?
  b The next train to Prague goes in ten minutes.
  c The clock said ten past two.
  d I bought two bedside tables and some red curtains.
  e We had fish soup and French bread.
  f Like most people, I sometimes feel lonely.

Reading: Left-handedness

1 a True
  b False
  c True (in the US)
  d True
  e False
  f False
  g False
  h True
2 The tusk it uses more is larger.
3 People don't have as much practice playing against left-handed players.
4 *b* and *f*.

Unit 14 The media

A Which page?

2 24	6 21–24	10 6–10	14 18
3 14	7 24	11 17	
4 2–5	8 11–12	12 15–16	
5 18	9 19–20	13 13	

C Understanding the headlines

1 The Mona Lisa has been stolen.
2 A new Shakespeare play has been discovered.
3 A bank manager has disappeared with £1 million.
4 A 12-year-old has climbed Mount Everest.
5 Electricity prices are going to rise by 150%.
6 The White House has been damaged by a bomb.
7 Britain will become a Republic on January 1.
8 A chimpanzee has won a game of chess.

Listening: Media habits

1 *Speaker 1*
  Newspaper: *The Scotsman*
  Magazines: *The Economist*
  TV: not much
  Radio: news, news discussion programmes
  Speaker 2
  Newspaper: *The Times*
  Magazines: *New Scientist*
  TV: movies, especially thrillers
  Radio: news, talk (not music)
2 a Both   e 2
  b 1   f 2
  c 2   g 1
  d Both

Phrasal verbs: Double meanings

1 give away   b, e   look up   i, k
  turn down   h, l   pick up   d, g
  bring up   c, f   put up   a, j
2 1 e   4 l   7 k   10 g
  2 b   5 f   8 i   11 j
  3 h   6 c   9 d   12 a
3 a … turned him down.
  b … look it up?
  c … give them away.
  d … put you up.
  e … turn it down?
  f … look him up?
  g … pick them up.
  h … brought me up.

Writing skills: Similarities

2 *Possible answers:*
  a Tobacco isn't very good for you, and nor is alcohol.
  b Both lions and wolves are dangerous animals.
  c Tokyo, Hong Kong and Singapore are all in the Far East.
  d Abraham Lincoln and John F Kennedy were both assassinated.
4 *Possible answers:*
  a John and Richard are both talented musicians. Both of them have good singing voices, and play several different instruments.
  b Neither Mars nor Jupiter is able to support life. Both planets are very cold, and neither of them has any oxygen in its atmosphere.

c Christianity, Islam and Buddhism are all major world religions which have spread through many countries. All three have millions of followers, and they have all had a major influence on art and literature.

Unit 15 Recent events

A Personal news

Possible answers:
1 We've finally arrived in Turkey. We got here yesterday morning. It wasn't a very good trip – we broke down twice! Anyway, we've found a lovely little apartment by the sea. The food's good, the sea's really warm, and everyone's very friendly.
2 I've given up smoking! I stopped two weeks ago. It was very difficult at first, but now it's getting much easier. Unfortunately, I'm putting on a lot of weight, but that's not important. The important thing is that I'm never going to smoke again.

B Asking questions

1 How did they get in?
  Have they been caught (yet)?
2 What caused the crash?
  Where did it happen?
  Were the people on board killed?
3 When did they arrive?
  How long did it take to get there?
  Have they sent back any photos?

C What have they been doing?

1 She's been writing letters.
2 They've been doing the housework / cleaning the flat.
3 He's been doing his homework.
4 They've been decorating their flat.
5 She's been getting ready to go out.
6 He's been playing chess.
7 She's been reading the paper.

Listening: What has happened?

1 *a* a party
  b a driving test
  c a car breaking down
2 1 – The woman's lost an earring.
    – Dancing.
    – He's going to look for it and ring her back.
  2 – Pleased/relieved. He's passed his driving test.
    – It's his third attempt to pass the test.
    – Go for a drive over the weekend.
  3 – The woman's car's broken down.
    – Borrow her friend's car. To pick someone up at the airport.
    – No. The friend says 'Oh not again' and 'You drove it last week, didn't you?'

Pronunciation: Changing stress

2 *a* – I've bought some chocolates.
  b – I've bought some chocolates.
  c – I've been on holiday.
  d – I've been on holiday.
  e – Do you want some orange juice?
  f – Do you want some orange juice?

Reading: Personal letters

1 Alan – writer
  Katrina – teacher
  Jim – musician (horn player)
2 *a* Alan   *d* Jim
  b Katrina   *e* Jim
  c Katrina, Alan *f* Katrina
3 *a* False   *f* True
  b False   *g* Can't tell
  c True   *h* False
  d False   *i* True
  e True

Unit 16 Teaching and learning

A School subjects

1 history   6 geography
2 music   7 biology
3 mathematics   8 languages
4 literature   9 chemistry
5 art   10 timetable

Listening: Three school subjects

1 B Latin names   H dates
  H famous people   H battles
  S equipment   B plants
  S experiment   H emperors
2 Speaker 1: *c*   Speaker 3: *b*
  Speaker 2: *d*   Speaker 4: *f*

Phrasal verbs: Prepositional verbs (1)

2 look after – care for
  look into – investigate
  call for – collect, pick up
  run into – meet (by chance)
  come across – find (by chance)
  take after – resemble
  take to – like, be attracted to
3 *a* take to   *e* take after
  b came across   *f* call for
  c look after   *g* ran into
  d looking into

Writing skills: Letter writing

1 *a* 5; *b* 2; *c* 4; *d* 3; *e* 1
2 *a* 1; *b* 5; *c* 3; *d* 4; *e* 2
3 A: 4; B: 1, 3; C: 2, 5

4 *Possible answers:*
1 Dear Sir/Madam,
I saw your advertisement for Banana T-shirts in the *Evening News*. Please send me two T-shirts, one medium and one large. I enclose a cheque for £30.
Yours faithfully,
2 Dear Sir/Madam,
I'm writing to ask for more information about your luxury campsites in Northern Spain. Please send me a brochure and details of prices and facilities available at the campsites. I look forward to hearing from you.
Yours faithfully,
3 Dear Mr Paterson,
I saw your advertisement in *Boats and Boating* this month, and I'm very interested in working on a yacht this summer. Please send me more information about the jobs you are offering, including details of pay and working conditions. I look forward to hearing from you soon.
Yours sincerely,

Unit 17 Narration

A What had happened?

Possible answers:
1 The train had left.
2 He had been shot.
3 Someone had locked it.
4 I had been arrested.
5 Someone had taken it.
6 He had had dinner there only the night before.
7 I had taken the bullets out.

B Past states and previous actions

Possible answers:
3 She had bruised her leg.
4 His hands were clean/washed.
5 Someone had switched on the light. / The light had been switched on.
6 The room was tidy.
7 The rain had stopped. / It had stopped raining.
8 They were asleep.

C Reported speech

2 … he/she wouldn't put up taxes.
3 … she had missed the last bus.
4 … they were doing all they could to solve the case.
5 … she didn't want to see him any more.
6 … I was going to have a fantastic week.
7 … he hadn't finished it yet.
8 … I would have to have an operation.

D I realised …

Possible answers:
1 It was two in the morning when Joe was woken up by a crash in the living room. He picked up the statue of Winston Churchill which he kept on his bedside table, and crept along the hall. Then he heard a 'miaow', and realised that it wasn't a burglar – it was the cat, which had knocked over a vase in the dark.
2 At last they were on the road. They'd packed all the suitcases, locked up their flat, and were on their way to the coast. In two hours, thought Helen, they would be on the ferry to France. She felt in her pocket – it was empty. And then she realised that she had left the tickets in the drawer in the hall. She sighed, and turned the car round.

Listening: Locked in!

1 *a* He was working alone in a room.
  b It was locked.
  c They'd switched the phones off for the weekend.
  d They wouldn't open.
  e There was a phone in there with a red light on.
2 cabinet; keys; matches; key; reception area; phone numbers; duty officer; phoned; let him out

Pronunciation: Linking words with /w/ or /j/

2 How interesting   /w/
  So am I   /w/
  My uncle   /j/
  Two or more   /w/
  Any others?   /j/
  High up in the sky /j/
  No overtaking   /w/
  Blue eyes   /w/

3 *a* They all /j/ went to Amsterdam. /w/
  b Who are /w/ you talking to on /w/ the phone?
  c Go up /w/ that way and /j/ you'll see it. /j/
  d He isn't /j/ very easy /j/ to talk to.
  e How many are /j/ there? Three or /j/ four?

Reading: Strange – but true?

1 *Suggested answers:*
  a Italy, USA
  b Australia, Bangladesh
  c Indonesia
  d Spain, Great Britain
  e Poland, USA

Unit 18 Breaking the law

A Criminals and their crimes

2 burglar   6 murderer
3 hijacker   7 shoplifter *Ladendieb*
4 smuggler   8 vandal
5 blackmailer   9 kidnapper

Possible crimes:
2 She broke into a house and stole a TV set and a video recorder.
3 He hijacked a plane on its way from London to New York and made the pilot fly to Beirut.
4 He smuggled 100 grams of heroin through customs hidden in a tube of toothpaste.

130 Answer key

5 She discovered that a colleague at work had been to prison, and told him she wanted £2,000 to keep quiet about it.
6 Her husband wouldn't give her a divorce, so she pushed him off a cliff.
7 He stole a camera from a department store.
8 She smashed windows in the local school and sprayed paint on the walls.
9 He kidnapped the baby son of a millionaire and demanded a ransom of $500,000.

B Crime story

arrested ... charged ... trial ... prosecution ... witnesses ... defence ... evidence ... jury ... verdict ... guilty ... judge ... fine ... prison ... court ... innocent

Listening: A case of fraud

2 *a* $10; family tree; family; famous / of interest; family tree
   b nothing of interest; family tree
3 After a time, he became *greedy*, and stopped *answering* letters. People in *each country* started to complain. They investigated, and *discovered* the man. The speaker thinks it's a pity he *was caught*.

Phrasal verbs: Prepositional verbs (2)

2 *a* 3; *b* 6; *c* 5; *d* 2; *e* 4; *f* 1
2 *a* went off   *d* getting over
   b cope with   *e* could do with
   c dealt with   *f* couldn't do without

Writing skills: Defining and non-defining relative clauses

2 *a* D
   b ND This is my friend Sarah, who I've known ...
   c D
   d D
   e ND Sydney, where I lived for ten years, is ...
   f D

3 *Possible answer:*
I was sitting in a café *where* I often go for a drink after work. I called the waiter, *who* I know quite well, *and* asked for a coffee and a ham sandwich. While I was waiting, I looked at a newspaper *which* was lying on the table, *and* started reading an article on the front page. It said, 'Police are looking for a medical student, Veronica Hall, *who* has been missing from her home for two weeks.' I looked at the photograph, *which* showed a young woman with dark, curly hair. It was a face I recognised at once. She was my new next-door neighbour, *who* had moved in just two weeks before.

Review Units 13–18

1 Sentence rewriting

1 I'm not quite as old as my brother. (I'm slightly younger than my brother.)
2 I can run much/far faster than you. (I'm a much faster runner than you.)
3 My son isn't tall enough to reach the light switch.
4 An escaped prisoner has been recaptured by the police.
5 He's not very good at typing.
6 She realised that they had already gone.
7 Someone had broken the window.

2 Verb forms

1 has been destroyed; started; spread; are still searching
2 I've been trying; I've given; have been doing (am doing); I've lost
3 had had; hadn't eaten; started

3 Vocabulary

1 comedy show – makes you laugh
  chat show – stars talking about themselves
  documentary – gives you information
  game show – trying to win prizes
  soap – never-ending drama
2 *a* history
  b geography
  c literature
  d mathematics (science, physics)
  e science
3 primary; secondary; degree; graduate
4 burglary; murderer; blackmail; vandal; robbery
5 the accused – the person on trial
  the defence – want a 'not guilty' verdict
  the judge – the person in charge
  the jury – decide on the verdict
  the prosecution – want a 'guilty' verdict
  the witnesses – give evidence

4 Fill the gaps

1 (news)paper; turn; told; would; had; be
2 wanted; having/taking; how; at; better
3 have; enough; much; to; cooked/made; been

6 Dictation

Yesterday morning, a woman walked into a charity shop carrying a large plastic sack. She told the assistant that it contained clothes that her family no longer needed. She handed over the sack and left.

Later on, she came back, and said that she had given them a coat belonging to her husband by mistake. The assistant explained that all the clothes that had been received that day had already been taken to the charity's head office for checking and cleaning, before being put on sale. The woman seemed very upset, and left immediately.

Meanwhile, an employee at head office was sorting through the sack of clothes when she discovered a number of rings, necklaces and other pieces of jewellery in the pocket of a man's coat. She called the police, and it turned out that the jewellery had been stolen from a local jeweller's shop in a robbery only the night before, and was worth nearly £300,000.

Police are now searching for the woman – and her husband – and expect to arrest them very soon.

Unit 19 Up to now

A Duration

1 *a* known; for   *b* been learning; for
  c had; since   *d* been playing; since
2 *a* Gary and Eileen have been engaged since July 1985.
  b Henry Palmer has been having driving lessons (has been learning to drive) for 20 years / since his 17th birthday.
  c Tom Kemp has been chewing (has had) the same piece of chewing gum for two years.
  d Ken Garret has been living in the garage since last October.
3 *a* They've been engaged since Eileen left school.
  b He's been having driving lessons since he was 17.
  c He's been chewing the same piece of chewing gum since he scored the winning goal in the Cup Final.
  d He's been living in the garage since he had an argument with his wife.

B How long (ago) …?

1 How long have you been living in Beverly Hills?
  How long ago did you make your first film?
2 How long ago did you join the company?
  How long have you been President?
Possible answers:
3 How long have you been playing with the band?
  How long ago did you learn to play the guitar?

Listening: Favourite things

1 a; photograph; beach; shorts and T-shirt
  b; camera; 12 years old; second-hand; outdated
  d; gramophone; wind-up; big horn
2 1 About ten years ago.
    The speaker and her sister.
    It's a nice memory.
  2 When he was 12 years old, in New York.
    He saved up for a year.
  3 Seven or eight years ago in Malaysia.
    It's beautiful, and it reminds him of Malaysia.

Pronunciation: Stress and suffixes

2 *a* politics   political
  b electric   electricity
  c mystery   mysterious
  d examined   examination
  e alcohol   alcoholic

Reading: Four logic puzzles

1 Quentin's; She's hurt her eye.
  (From left to right, the patients are: Richard, Quentin, Ursula, Tom, Sue.)
2 Three years; he's 33.
3 Alice and Cecil live on Alithia; they've been married for nine years, and have three children.
  Brian and Delia live on Pseudia; they've been married for ten years and have one child.

4 | Jim | Kate | Laura | Mike |
|---|---|---|---|
| teacher | electrician | doctor | baker |
| 2 years | 1 year | 4 years | 3 years |
| 1 week ago | 1 week ago | 2 weeks ago | 2 weeks ago |
| Kate | Jim | Mike | Laura |
| lost | won | won | lost |

Unit 20 In your lifetime

A ⎡F⎤⎡r⎤⎡o⎤⎡m⎤ ⎡c⎤⎡r⎤⎡a⎤⎡d⎤⎡l⎤⎡e⎤ ⎡t⎤⎡o⎤ ⎡g⎤⎡r⎤⎡a⎤⎡v⎤⎡e⎤

mid*wi*fe; bi*r*th; b*o*rn; *m*other
*c*hristened
b*r*ides; m*a*rried; we*d*ding; re*l*igious; offic*e*
  recep*t*ion; honeymo*o*n
ag*e*; bu*r*ied; cr*e*mated; hea*v*en; funeral

C What are they like?

1 naughty   4 lonely   7 shy
2 ambitious   5 self-conscious 8 helpless
3 wise   6 independent   9 rebellious

Listening: Birth and marriage

1 B trapeze act   A Russians
  A pregnant   A swimming pool
  B groom   B circus tent
  A midwife   B bride
  B clowns   A hospital
  A pain   B reception
2 *a* … in water.
  b … you don't feel any pain.
  c … little swimming pool.
  d … midwife.
  e … had a baby girl.
  f … get married in a circus.
  g … in fancy dress.
  h … did a trapeze act.
  i … rehearsing/practising.

Phrasal verbs: Three-word verbs (1)

2 *a* … on cigarettes.
  b … with my work.
  c … for cars.
  d … with the others.
  e … of sugar.
3 *a* catch up with
  b cut down on
  c look out for
  d get on with
  e run out of

Writing skills: Joining ideas: showing what's coming next

1 a5; b3; c2
2 *a* Fortunately
  b Not surprisingly
  c Surprisingly
  d On the other hand
  e On the contrary / In fact
  f On the contrary / In fact
  g Unfortunately

3 *Possible answers:*
   a ... she works very hard.
   b ... she turned him down.
   c ... a landrover came by and pulled them back into town.
   d ... the work's very interesting.
   e ... it was closed while I was there.

Unit 21 Finding out

A Questions

2 What (sort/kind of clothes) shall I wear?
3 How long did it take you to find the house?
4 What kind/sort/brand of toothpaste do you use?
5 How often do they visit the States?
6 How much (money) did you have with you?
7 What flavour chewing gum do you like best?
8 How far is your flat from the centre? / How far from the centre is your flat?

B They don't know ...

They don't know what he was typing when he died.
They don't know how the murderer knew that he would be there.
They don't know what the murderer hit him with.
They don't know if/whether Sir Hugh knew the murderer (or not).
They don't know where the murderer has hidden the murder weapon.
They don't know if/whether the murderer is still in the house (or not).
They don't know who killed Sir Hugh.

C Reported questions

2 ... if/whether she would pick him up from the office after work.
3 ... how long he had been waiting.
4 ... when he/she would be back from lunch.
5 ... how much he had in his account.
6 ... if/whether he had cleaned his teeth.
7 ... if/whether he could have the day off on Friday.
8 ... when the world was going to end.

D Question tags

1 El Greco wasn't Greek, was he?
2 You haven't met the Prime Minister, have you?
3 He was arrested for shoplifting, wasn't he?
4 He's a bit strange, isn't he?
5 She's always losing her handbag, isn't she?
6 Ostriches can't fly, can they?
7 You won't tell anyone, will you?

Listening: Phone conversation

1 – Someone in a computer repair shop.
   – Her printer, which isn't working.
   – The motor has burnt out.
2 *See tapescript.*

Pronunciation: Changing tones

2 a He's studying French ↘ at university. ↗
   b He's studying French ↘ at university. ↘
   c No. We got married ↘ on Saturday. ↘
   d No. I stayed at home ↘ last night. ↗
   e Oh, I see him ↗ almost every day. ↘

Reading: A bit of luck

1 a In a station bookstall.
   b That he didn't know anything about her.
2 – He realises she must have come from the west side of the station, so he can find out what buses would take her there.
   – He saw the *Nursing Journal*, and realised she was a nurse.
   – She hadn't had coffee since 4 (a.m.) – so she'd been on night duty.
   – He finds Zena Yates in the hospital, and through her finds the woman.
3 Something like 'Have you lent a suitcase to anyone recently?'
4 Valeria Watson.

Unit 22 Speaking personally

A Three ways of talking about feelings

1
depress	depressed	*depressing*
embarrass	*embarrassed*	embarrassing
excite	excited	*exciting*
frighten	frightened	*frightening*
relax	*relaxed*	*relaxing*
upset	*upset*	upsetting
worry	*worried*	*worrying*

2 b embarrassing   g upset
  c frightened   h embarrassed
  d depressed   i worry
  e relax   j relaxing
  f frightens (worries); exciting

C Good and bad

1 brilliant; terrific; wonderful
2 awful; dreadful; terrible
3 a boring   c exciting
  b amusing, entertaining   d disappointing
4 fascinating

Listening: James Bond films

2 a 2, 3   e 2
  b 2   f 1
  c 3   g 1
  d 3
3 a I've grown out of them.
    The gadgets ... seem ridiculous to our generation.
  b pure escapism
    you can switch off

c (it had) brilliant theme music
they followed the books pretty closely

Phrasal verbs: Three-word verbs (2)

1 a put up with
  b look out on
  c get down to
  d look up to
  e look down on
  f stand up for
3 a looks up to
  b got down to
  c looks down on
  d looks out on
  e put up with
  f stood up for

Writing skills: Sequence: unexpected events

1 Normal sequence of events: *1a, 2a, 3a*.
  Something sudden and unexpected: *1b, 2b, 3b*.
2 *Possible answers:*
  a He was just about to drink the wine ...
  b After the waiter brought her the change ...
  c I was just getting on the bus ...
  d He'd just put the cake in the oven ...
  e Before I went into the flat ...
3 *Possible anwer:*
I'd just come home when the telephone rang. A voice said, 'Meet me downstairs in ten minutes – it's important.' I put my coat on, and I was just going out of the door when the phone rang again. The same voice said, 'Walk straight across the street to the other side.' While I was crossing the street, I heard the sound of a car accelerating. I ran as fast as I could and I'd just reached the pavement when a Mercedes drove past, missing me by inches.

Unit 23 The unreal past

A What would you have done?

Possible answers:
1 I wouldn't have carried on reading my paper.
  I would have complained / walked out.
2 I would have told him to stop it.
  I would have sent him out of the room.
3 I would have waited for her.
  I would have helped her with her suitcases.
4 I would have tried to suck out the poison.
  I would have walked slowly – I wouldn't have run.

B Third conditionals

Possible answers:
1 ... if I had had enough money.
2 ... I wouldn't have offered them lamb curry.
3 If that woman hadn't shouted ...
4 ... if you hadn't left it on the pavement.
5 ... it wouldn't have bitten you.
6 If he'd said that to me ...
7 ... if they'd had some better music.

C It's all your fault

Possible answers:
1 If you'd got here sooner ...
2 If you'd packed some blankets, we wouldn't be so cold.
  If you'd filled up with petrol, we'd be home by now.
3 If you'd worn a mask, we wouldn't be in prison.
  If you hadn't dropped the money, we'd be having the time of our lives in Las Vegas.
4 If you'd brought the right equipment, we wouldn't be lying here covered in bandages.
  If you'd been more careful, we'd be on the top of the mountain watching the sun go down.

D It's all my own fault

Possible answers:
2 I wish I'd brought some warm clothes.
  I should have filled up with petrol.
  I wish we'd stayed at home.
3 I wish we'd never robbed the bank.
  We should have planned it more carefully.
  I wish we'd managed to get to Las Vegas.
4 We should have taken the proper equipment.
  I wish we'd chosen an easier mountain.
  I shouldn't have been so careless.

Listening: A better place

1 We should *listen* to *other people*.
  We should get our power from *water* instead of *oil*.
  Men should have *babies*.
  Cars produce *exhaust* fumes.
  Guns cause a huge number of *injuries*.
2 1*a*; 2*b*; 3*b*; 4*b*; 5*a*

Reading: If things had been different ...

a False
b False
c False
d Can't tell
e True
f False
g True
h False
i True
j True
k False
l False
m Can't tell

Unit 24 Life on Earth

A Environment quiz

1 global
2 rain
3 ozone
4 power
5 nuclear
6 chemicals
7 carbon
8 pollution
9 Sahara
10 forest
11 greenhouse

Listening: How green are you?

1

	1	2	3
buy 'green' products	✔	?	✔
don't waste paper	✘	✔	✔
don't waste plastic	✘	?	✔
avoid car travel	✘	✘	✔
recycle glass/paper	?	✔	✔
Possible score	2–3	4–6	7–9

2 1 She doesn't buy products if they've got CFC gases.
  She doesn't take her own bag shopping; she keeps getting new ones from shops.
 2 He doesn't run the tap while he's cleaning his teeth.
  He turns the heating up rather than put on a jumper.

3 All the waste paper is collected and recycled.
She doesn't recycle cans – just throws them away.

Phrasal verbs: Review

1 *a* ... on our journey. *e* ... from the station.
  b ... to my homework. *f* ... on a large lake.
  c ... the answer. *g* ... some new clothes.
  d ... their baby. *h* ... an old friend.
2 *a* ... let me down. *e* ... give them away.
  b ... took off. *f* ... do without her.
  c ... deal with them. *g* ... put up with her/it?
  d ... catch up with them. *h* ... gets over it soon.

Writing skills: Organising ideas

1 They show more clearly how the second and third sentences are connected to the first. They make it clear that the writer is talking about an *advantage* of word-processors, and about *reasons* for the disappearance of frogs and toads.
2 *Possible answers:*
  a The (only) result will be that even more people will travel by car ...
  b The (main) reason was that the Indians ...
  c The problem is that they need at least ...
  d The only problem is that it uses up ...
  e The main advantage is that I can work ...
3 *Possible continuations:*
  a A better solution would be to improve bus services and build an underground railway.
  b Another reason was that the white settlers had better weapons and a more organised army.
  c They can also be very noisy, which is very annoying for the neighbours.
  d Also, I often get stopped by the police, and have to pay fines for speeding.
  e If I feel like it, I can take a week off work, or I can decide to work over the weekend.

Review Units 19–24

1 Sentence rewriting

1 I've had this typewriter since I left school.
2 They've been watching TV for four hours.
3 It's 500 years since the volcano (last) erupted.
4 I've no idea where she lives.
5 He asked me whether I'd locked the front door.
6 If I'd had enough money, I would have bought it.
7 I wish I'd apologised.

2 Asking questions

1 How long have you been learning Chinese?
2 You haven't seen my glasses, have you?
3 What flavour (ice-cream) would you like?
4 What make of car have you got / do you have / do you drive?
5 How long does it take to get there by bus?
6 Could you tell me the way to the station / how to get to the station / where the station is?
7 Penguins live at the North Pole, don't they?

3 Vocabulary

1 *Birth:* christen, midwife
  Marriage: bridegroom, honeymoon, reception
  Death: cemetery, coffin, funeral, mourning
2 ambitious – wants to be Prime Minister
  naughty – behaves like a child
  self-conscious – gets embarrassed easily
  rebellious – dislikes authority
  wise – knows a lot about life
3 *Possible answers:*
  a worried *c* depressed
  b relaxed *d* excited
4 entertaining – amusing
  dull – boring
  terrible – dreadful
  terrific – brilliant
  interesting – fascinating
5 *a* Acid *d* rainforests; extinct
  b layer *e* power
  c greenhouse; global

4 Fill the gaps

1 allowed; fight/die; enough; law
2 was; when; how; been; for; would; refused; get; off/away
3 hit; have; become; human; much/far; than

6 Dictation

I saw a fantastic horror film last night. It was all about a village where strange creatures were attacking young people at night and carrying them off. No-one knew what they were, or why they were doing it. But the attacks always happened near the cemetery, and people started to believe that the creatures were dead bodies which were coming out of their graves.

Anyway, one girl managed to get away when she was attacked, and she said she thought the creature had recognised her and let her go.

And in the end it turned out that the creature was her grandfather, who lived in an old people's home near the church. This mad doctor who ran the home had discovered a way to make old people young again, using blood taken from teenagers, and he was giving these elderly people an amazing drug which temporarily turned them into monsters, and was sending them out at night to catch teenagers for his experiments. But when the old man saw his granddaughter, he realised what was happening, and told the others. And they attacked the mad scientist and killed him. It was really enjoyable.

Phrasal verbs: reference

Introduction

Phrasal verbs have two parts: a *verb* (e.g. *make, go, get*) and a *'small word'* (e.g. *on, up, out, with*). This 'small word' may be an adverb or a preposition. Some phrasal verbs (Type 4, below) have two 'small words'.

Types of phrasal verb

Type 1: *Verb + adverb* (Units 4, 6)

take off	The plane *took off*.
get up	I *get up* at 6 o'clock.

These verbs are intransitive (they have no object).

Type 2: *Verb + noun + adverb* (Units 8, 10, 12, 14)

take … off	He *took* his shoes *off*.
give … away	She *gave* all her money *away*.

These verbs are transitive (they have an object: *shoes, money*).

If the object is a noun, the adverb can come *before* or *after* it. So we can say:

He *took* his shoes *off*.   or
He *took off* his shoes.

If the object is a pronoun (*him, her, it, them*), the adverb must come *after* it. So we can say:

He *took* them *off*.   but not ~~He took off them~~.

Type 3: *Verb + preposition + noun* (Units 16, 18)

look for	I'm *looking for* my glasses.
take after	She *takes after* her mother.

These are sometimes called 'prepositional verbs'. The preposition (*for, after,* etc.) must come *before* the noun. (We cannot say ~~I'm looking my glasses for.~~)

Type 4: *Verb + adverb + preposition + noun* (Units 20, 22)

run out of	I've *run out of* matches.
get down to	It's time to *get down to* some work.

These are sometimes called 'three-word verbs'. They are a combination of Types 1 and 3.

The meanings of phrasal verbs

With some phrasal verbs, the meaning is obvious:

He *got in* the car and *drove off*.
He *turned round* and saw me.

But many phrasal verbs have an 'idiomatic' meaning which cannot easily be guessed from the individual words:

They *turned up* an hour later (= arrived).
She *made* the story *up* (= invented).
I'm trying to *cut down on* cigarettes (= smoke less).

Some common 'idiomatic' phrasal verbs with their meanings

Type 1

carry on	=	continue
find out	=	discover
grow up	=	become adult
set off	=	start (a journey)
settle down	=	live in one place
take off	=	leave the ground
turn up	=	arrive (unexpectedly)

Type 2

bring sg. up	=	introduce (a topic)
bring s.o. up	=	raise (a child)
give sg. away	=	reveal (a secret); give (for no money)
give sg. up	=	stop (doing)
let s.o. down	=	disappoint
look sg. up	=	find the meaning (of a word)
look s.o. up	=	visit (after a long time)
make sg./s.o. out	=	understand
make sg. up	=	invent
pick sg. up	=	take (from the ground)
pick s.o. up	=	collect, meet
put s.o. down	=	criticise/humiliate
put sg. off	=	delay, postpone
put sg. up	=	build, construct
put s.o. up	=	have to stay (as a guest)
ring s.o. up	=	telephone
run sg./s.o. over	=	drive over (in a car)
take sg. up	=	start (doing)
talk s.o. round	=	persuade
think sg. over	=	consider carefully
turn s.o./sg. down	=	refuse
turn sg. up/down	=	make louder/quieter
work sg. out	=	find the answer (to a problem)

Type 3

call for sg./s.o.	=	collect
come across sg.	=	find (by chance)
cope with sg.	=	manage
deal with sg.	=	be concerned with
(could) do with sg.	=	would like
(can't) do without sg./s.o.	=	need
get over sg.	=	recover from
go off sg./s.o.	=	stop liking
look after sg./s.o.	=	care for, be responsible for
look into sg.	=	investigate
run into s.o.	=	meet (by chance)
take after s.o.	=	resemble (an older relative)
take to sg./s.o.	=	like, be attracted to

Type 4

catch up with sg./s.o.	=	draw level with
cut down on sg.	=	reduce the amount of
get down to sg.	=	start doing
get on with sg.	=	make progress with, continue
get on with s.o.	=	like being with
look down on s.o.	=	despise
look out for sg./s.o.	=	watch for, be careful of
look out on sg.	=	have a view of
look up to s.o.	=	respect
put up with sg./s.o.	=	tolerate
run out of sg.	=	have no more of
stand up for sg./s.o.	=	defend

sg.= something   s.o.= someone